Hannah Anderson's meditations in *Turning of Days* capture my heart at the core. It is like a walk in the woods with the Scriptures. Her words come to life on the pages, enhanced further by the natural images. It is like a flashing yellow-light invitation to slow down and drink deep of God's goodness right here in this wild world he has made. *Turning of Days* is a worthy celebration of beauty that comes at just the right time.

SANDRA MCCRACKEN | Singer and songwriter, *Patient Kingdom*

This book left us breathless. It powerfully knits the threads of natural revelation and grace, and reflects the consistently holistic way our loving Creator reveals Himself. Hannah's stunning writing and Nathan's delightful illustrations elevated what we get to call our daily work in a way that will never leave us.

SARAH AND STEVE PABODY | CEOs, Triple Wren Farms

Gracefully written essays turn gently with the seasons. Each opens with an experience in nature and ends with relevant teachings of Scripture. Anderson's writing is intimate, moody, soothing; at times searing, like nature and life itself.

JULIE ZICKEFOOSE | Author and illustrator, *The Bluebird Effect* and *Saving Jemima*

As soon as I finished reading *Turning of Days*, I went back to start reading it again. There is an abundance of searching, patient wisdom here, drawn from things we always see but rarely notice, and written in beautiful prose. Read, and enjoy.

ANDREW WILSON | Teaching Pastor, King's Church London

Christians throughout the centuries have affirmed what the Wisdom Literature of Holy Scripture states bluntly: that if we had ears to hear and eyes to see, we would discover in creation an alphabet of theology, or as the Reformer John Calvin once put it: how the little birds that sing, sing of God, how the beasts clamor for Him, how the elements dread Him, how the mountains echo Him, and how the flowers laugh before Him. This, too, is what Hannah Anderson invites us to discover in her beautiful series of reflections on nature: the ways of God in the works of God so that we might revel in the wonder of God. As a theologian and an artist, we loved this book, with its delightful illustrations by Nathan Anderson, and we hope many others do too!

DAVID AND PHAEDRA TAYLOR | David is Associate Professor of Theology and Culture, Fuller Theological Seminary and author of *Open and Unafraid*; Phaedra is an artist and gardener

Turning of Days brings reminders that will both inspire and comfort you. You'll be reminded of God's faithfulness through His Word, displayed in nature.

RUTH CHOU SIMONS | Founder of gracelaced.com; bestselling author of *GraceLaced and Beholding* and *Becoming*; coauthor of *Foundations*

The apostle Paul tells us that God's eternal power and divine nature can be clearly seen through the world around us. But it is often hard to read nature's testimony, for we've forgotten the vocabulary. But *Turning of Days* is a delightful primer for us all. Take and read! After that, get yourself a little blank book and pencils then take a long, slow walk outside and transcribe creation around you—as is so delightfully modeled for you in these pages.

NED BUSTARD | Illustrator and designer of *Every Moment Holy*

Turning *of* Days

Lessons from Nature, Season, and Spirit

HANNAH ANDERSON

with illustrations by Nathan Anderson

MOODY PUBLISHERS

CHICAGO

All Scripture quotations, unless otherwise indicated, are taken from the Holy Bible, New International Version®, NIV®. Copyright © 1973, 1978, 1984, 2011 by Biblica, Inc.™ Used by permission of Zondervan. All rights reserved worldwide. www.zondervan.com The "NIV" and "New International Version" are trademarks registered in the United States Patent and Trademark Office by Biblica, Inc.™

Scripture quotations marked CSB have been taken from the Christian Standard Bible®, Copyright © 2017 by Holman Bible Publishers. Used by permission. Christian Standard Bible® and CSB® are federally registered trademarks of Holman Bible Publishers.

Scripture quotations marked (ESV) are from The ESV® Bible (The Holy Bible, English Standard Version®), copyright © 2001 by Crossway, a publishing ministry of Good News Publishers. Used by permission. All rights reserved.

Scripture quotations marked NASB are taken from the New American Standard Bible® (NASB), Copyright © 1960, 1962, 1963, 1968, 1971, 1972, 1973, 1975, 1977, 1995 by The Lockman Foundation. Used by permission. www.Lockman.org.

Scripture quotations marked NKJV are taken from the New King James Version®. Copyright © 1982 by Thomas Nelson. Used by permission. All rights reserved.

Scripture quotations marked KJV are taken from the King James Version.

All emphasis in Scripture has been added.

Details of some stories have been changed to protect the privacy of individuals.

Published in association with the literary agency of Wolgemuth & Associates.

Edited by Amanda Cleary Eastep
Interior and cover design: Erik M. Peterson
Cover and interior illustrations by Nathan Anderson

All websites and phone numbers listed herein are accurate at the time of publication but may change in the future or cease to exist. The listing of website references and resources does not imply publisher endorsement of the site's entire contents. Groups and organizations are listed for informational purposes, and listing does not imply publisher endorsement of their activities.

Library of Congress Cataloging-in-Publication Data

Names: Anderson, Hannah, 1979- author. | Anderson, Nathan (Illustrator),
   illustrator.
Title: Turning of days : lessons from nature, season, and spirit / Hannah
   Anderson ; text illustrations by Nathan Anderson.
Description: Chicago : Moody Publishers, [2021] | Includes bibliographical
   references. | Summary: "Turning of Days beckons you to a world of tree
   frogs and peach blossoms, mountain springs and dark winter nights-all in
   search of nature's God, all in harmony with Scripture. Join Hannah
   Anderson, author of Humble Roots, as she journeys through the four
   seasons in this collection of devotional essays and illustrations. Take
   a look, and see His glory everywhere"-- Provided by publisher.
Identifiers: LCCN 2020036763 (print) | LCCN 2020036764 (ebook) | ISBN
   9780802418562 | ISBN 9780802497376 (ebook)
Subjects: LCSH: Creation--Miscellanea. | Seasons--Religious
   aspects--Christianity--Miscellanea.
Classification: LCC BS652 .A64 2021 (print) | LCC BS652 (ebook) | DDC
   231.7/65--dc23
LC record available at https://lccn.loc.gov/2020036763
LC ebook record available at https://lccn.loc.gov/2020036764

Originally delivered by fleets of horse-drawn wagons, the affordable paperbacks from D. L. Moody's publishing house resourced the church and served everyday people. Now, after more than 125 years of publishing and ministry, Moody Publishers' mission remains the same—even if our delivery systems have changed a bit. For more information on other books (and resources) created from a biblical perspective, go to www.moodypublishers.com or write to:

Moody Publishers
820 N. LaSalle Boulevard
Chicago, IL 60610

1 3 5 7 9 10 8 6 4 2

Printed in the United States of America

To our parents who chose the land
and raised us close to it.
We love it because you loved it first.
HRA & NDA

Contents

From the Author

THIS BOOK IS A BIT OF A PARADOX because it attempts to use words where nature doesn't. Writing it was no less paradoxical, and I imagine reading it will be as well. The primary paradox, of course, is that God chooses to reveal Himself through both the natural world and the Holy Scriptures. He chooses to make Himself known through both the universal and the specific. He is the God of both common and particular grace.

Those accustomed to knowing God in certain ways may find it challenging to encounter Him in different ones. Perhaps you'll ask, "What can nature teach me about God that Scripture cannot?" or "If I can meet God on a mountain top, why should I worry about a book?" But let me suggest different questions: "What will you miss if you don't encounter God in all the ways He chooses to reveal Himself? What will you miss if you don't embrace the paradox of revelation?"

In Psalm 19, David writes that the heavens declare the glory of God and that the precepts of the Lord give joy to the heart; and with this, David shows us how to love both the works and words of God. More than metaphor, the natural world is a living, pulsating experience of truth that surrounds and enfolds us, teaching us deep realities without words. And more than a mandate, the Scripture is a stable source of truth standing outside and apart from us, teaching us those realities that exist beyond nature's shifts and time's evolutions. Together, both reveal the Divine.

Ultimately, we must embrace the paradox, learning from nature what it must tell us and learning from Scripture what it must tell us. But if God is the God of both nature and Scripture, do not be surprised when they say the same thing. Do not be surprised when they sing in harmony.

One final note: I wrote this book as a collection of devotional essays (rather than in my typical book-length form) because I want to invite you to slow down and reflect on nature's testimony. Of course, you're welcome to read it straight through, from beginning to end, but you may find yourself frustrated by a lack of narrative arc and neat resolution. Instead you'll find a collection of vignettes and sketches roughly organized around the four seasons as we experience them in the mountains of Virginia. I chose this form to invite you into a way of seeing the natural world by modeling observation and repetition over time. I suppose you might say I'm inviting you into a kind of field work.

As you read and reflect, I hope you'll begin to understand the deep truths that shape our days and years on this earth. If I've done my job, you'll encounter both wonder and fear. Beauty and horror. Visible and invisible. You will be enlarged and brought low, drawn close and kept at a distance. I hope you'll find yourself more comfortable with the paradox that is life and, perhaps, even more at peace with the God who gave it to you. But more than anything, I hope you'll discover a new way of perceiving creation and learn, with poet William Blake, how "to see a World in a Grain of Sand/And a Heaven in a Wild Flower."[1]

Venturing Out

"But ask the animals, and they will teach you, or the birds in the sky, and they will tell you; or speak to the earth, and it will teach you, or let the fish in the sea inform you. Which of all these does not know that the hand of the LORD has done this? In his hand is the life of every creature and the breath of all mankind."

JOB 12:7—10

I WALKED IN THE WOODS today, and it made me wonder why I walk anywhere else. It's not quite spring, but spring is coming. I know it; the birds know it; the trees know it; and the small sprigs of green sprouting between the leaves on the forest floor know it. But spring is not here yet.

It's late February. The air is cool, and a thick cloud cover lends the river a celadon hue. It's a sickly color that doesn't reflect tree or sky or human face as rivers should and is, instead, wholly absorbed in itself, flowing confidently as it gathers raindrops to carry downstream. When I left the house, it was not raining, but by the time I hit the path, I had turned up my collar and thrust my hands into my pockets. It's hard to walk this way, hunched over and closed in on yourself. Let me restate that: It's not hard to *walk* this way—my legs and feet work just fine and tramp easily along the path by the river—but it is hard to *see* this way. It is hard to see what you're supposed to see. It's hard to see what the world is meant to teach you when you're balled up into yourself and all your attention is given to resisting the elements.

But then the rain stops. The clouds don't quite lift, but the rain stops. I relax my shoulders and lift my eyes. I look. I listen. I see.

To my right, a pair of white-breasted nuthatches perch in a thicket. One is screaming to the other: "Fly! Fly! A stranger is coming. Fly! Fly! A stranger is here!"

But I'm no stranger. Not really. Still, I know that they'll only find peace in my absence, so I continue down the trail to where it cuts away from the river about fifty yards on. Here, I'm hidden from the birds who sit in the branches that hang over the swollen water. I stop and lower myself onto my haunches and disappear even further in the brush. Maybe if I'm quiet, I can see without being seen.

And so I stay there, stretched on my quadriceps for five, ten, fifteen minutes, my eyes and ears waiting. I see a flash of color and hear the whir of a cardinal's flight. I listen to the steady beat of a woodpecker and see her downy head drum, drum, drumming against a branch. There's a rustle to my left. I turn, but I'm not quick enough and just barely see a chipmunk's rump, striped and round. But I see it.

Congratulating myself, I walk on until I can see daffodils blooming where a house once stood. There's a rock wall across the way and a row of stones lined up straight. A tree grows up through the middle of them. Then, as if the woods need me to know that my own kind thrived here too, a man with a brush mustache and two small dogs emerges on the trail. He stops, and I kneel again, this time to a chorus of yips and yelps that welcome me as a friend. He tells me that he used to swim in the river and knows its fish. He points to a small island in the green water and tells me of a tree that grew there once but doesn't now.

We say goodbye and be safe, and I trade the trail along the river for one that veers straight up the hillside deeper into the woods. The leaves lie thick on the path and don't crunch when I walk on them because they are varnished with rain. I worry for a moment that I'll slip and tumble down the hillside. The hills become dangerous when they're wet: water and inclined planes being no friends. I see mature trees lying on their sides, a hundred and a hundred-and-fifty feet long, their ends turned up in spiraling clumps of mud, rock, and root. They've been brought down by the rain and sodden ground. Drip by drip, drop by drop, the water pulled away and reshaped the landscape that sustained them until a passing wind or coat of ice toppled the mightiest.

Roots or no roots, they lie flat on the ground, humbled for their journey back to the soil. They become shelter for salamanders and snails and food for beetles and termites. Their bark crumbles and falls off. Fungus grows: red, golden, shelf-like, and magnificent.

All because of the rain that rolls down like justice, reshaping and reforming the land and everything in its path. So I worry about water and slick leaves because water is a powerful thing, but ultimately, my worry is pointless. I do not slip. I do not fall on the path and even find a way to navigate the trees that did. One day, someone will come with a chainsaw and oil can and clear the trail, but today I'll find my own way.

The trees that do stand are still bare, their limbs so many bones. In any other season, they'd be clothed in leaves, their nakedness covered like that of the first man and woman. But like them, these leaves were also sure to fall. So here, on this almost-spring-not-yet-spring morning, I can only know the trees by their fruit. I see the pine cones and the spiked balls of the sycamore still clinging to the highest branches. The black walnuts—whose husks stained my grandmother's hands as she gathered them—lie on the ground in front of me. For a moment, I'm tempted to pick one up and carry it home in my empty pocket; but not willing to get my hands dirty, I don't.

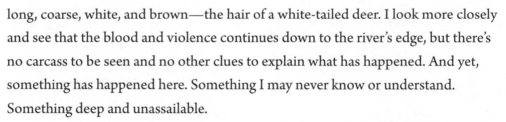

Too soon, my path circles back to the river, but as quickly as I emerge, I stop. Large clumps of hair and pink flesh litter the trail in front of me. The hair is long, coarse, white, and brown—the hair of a white-tailed deer. I look more closely and see that the blood and violence continues down to the river's edge, but there's no carcass to be seen and no other clues to explain what has happened. And yet, something has happened here. Something I may never know or understand. Something deep and unassailable.

My mind whirls with all it knows and all it doesn't. There are mysteries in this world, not just of science but of conscience. Mysteries of unity and continuity, of both wonder and groaning, of creation awaiting redemption. What might I observe were I to crouch down low and turn my eyes and tune my ears? What might I discover of pain and loss, of beauty and truth? What might I find were I to drop my shoulders, lift my head, and keep watch in this world? What might I learn if I asked the earth to teach me?

SCRIPTURE

Job 12:7–10 | Psalm 19:104

Spring

I.

SPRING IN APPALACHIA is a strange mix of hope and persistence. The dark, dreary days of winter do not go easily, and spring comes in on a dance of two steps forward and one back. But soon enough, the mud and slog and slosh are replaced by bits of green and yellow. The crocuses and forsythia bloom, and the trees bud with those at the base of the mountains coming into color first. And slowly, steadily, spring works its way up the ridges and crests in the same hues that, come autumn, will cause the hills to burst into full flame.

But like any lover, an Appalachian spring will flirt with you, testing and trying your commitment. One moment all will be heat and light with a cloudy chill descending the next. We only know spring is serious in its affections when we hear the faint, sweet mating calls of the tree frogs that make their home in our waterways. Weighing just over a one-tenth of an ounce and only an inch long, these "spring peepers" (*Pseudacris crucifer*) fill the evenings with an ever expanding chorus of hope. Spring is not yet here, but there's no stopping it now.

And yet, as I've come to learn, an Appalachian spring is a particular thing, and the call of spring peepers is not universally understood.

I grew up in the mountains of southwest Pennsylvania, just over the border from West Virginia, but I spent my college years in the southern United States and found myself particularly homesick during the spring. What I knew to be a lilting waltz with a coy partner was, there, a quick step and one headlong plunge into the arms of the sweat and humidity of summer.

The spring of my sophomore year, my homesickness was compounded by a larger sense of alienation. My new friends and classmates had no reference for gray skies that give way to blue, frozen ground that gradually softens, or streams that run heavy with snow melt. And any mention of spring peepers was met with quizzical looks and the assumption that I was talking about baby chicks. Or worse, Easter candy. I was young enough to regard this as more than sufficient proof of my uniqueness, undeniable confirmation that I was alone in the world.

Until one evening.

I'd just finished dinner with a boy I'd recently met, and we were walking to the library where I worked. We were still getting to know each other, but in my current mood, I wasn't interested in much more. He told me he'd been raised in the mountains of southwest Virginia, further south than where I'd grown up, but not so far south as to not know what spring should look like. Being testy, I decided to test him.

"You know what I miss most about spring?" I baited, "I miss spring peepers."

His answer was immediate and sure, this slightly-awkward religion major dressed in mismatched hand-me-downs.

"Me too. Especially this time of night when they're just starting to sing."

Not too long ago, I drove this boy's truck along a winding mountain road on my way home from church. It was already dark, and I could trace my headlights in the fog that hovers and crawls "on little cat feet"[2] across the mountains. Approaching a narrow bridge that straddles a creek, I slowed, and I heard them. I heard those tiny warblers singing their chorus of hope and desire. I heard the sound of love in Appalachia.

If I'm honest, I never expected to live in these mountains. For that matter, I really never expected to marry. And never once did I guess that my first step toward my present life would include spring peepers.

Whenever I'm tempted to doubt God's providence, whenever I'm tempted to think that I somehow missed the life I was supposed to have, when the hard times come and the pain bears down, I remember spring peepers. And I think of how God reveals Himself and His will. He doesn't shout His plans from the mountains so much as He repeats them over and over in low, quiet songs that only make sense to those who know the significance of them. Like spring in Appalachia, His plans unfold in gentle, persistent ways—sometimes two steps forward and one back—but always in rhythm and always in time.

And I think of ancient Eliezer, looking for a bride, and how being in the way, the Lord led him. I think of how we all plan our steps, but God cuts the path. How He

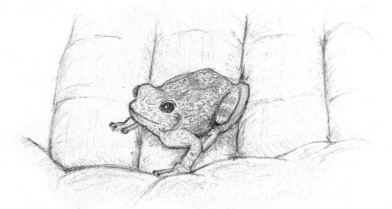

intermingles all the things that we consider inconsequential, all the things that have shaped and molded us, all our pain and all our delight, to bring about our good and make us the same.

So I idle the truck for a moment, there on the bridge, and roll down my windows to listen to the sound of an Appalachian spring. I listen to those tiny frogs sing of providence and goodness and drawing love. I listen, and for this moment at least, all my questions and all my doubts are silenced in the chorus. I listen, and then I make my way home.

SCRIPTURE

Genesis 24; 50:20 | Proverbs 3:5–6; 16:9; 20:24 | Romans 8:28–29

II.

*"Now the LORD God had planted a garden in the east, in Eden;
and there he put the man he had formed."*

GENESIS 2:8

WE'VE JUST TURNED OVER the garden and started talking about what will go in
and when. We don't have a large plot—not by most people's imaginations anyway—
but it's enough to grow in, and I'm always amazed by how little land is needed. At least
according to the magazine I get that tells me how to produce a year's worth of food on
an acre. Obviously, some crops, like corn or wheat, require more space, and heaven
help you if you don't stake your tomatoes. But with good planning and better tending,
a garden requires less land than you might think. In fact, one of nature's private jokes
is that we generally only use 6–12 inches of soil to garden. We literally scratch the
surface of this planet to grow our beans, carrots, and cucumbers. And while I love the
biology of it, I love the geometry more: the layering of crops and reclaiming soil in raised
beds and containers. I love how good stewardship can bring abundance from little.

So I'm out in our little patch this afternoon thinking that dirt is a wondrous thing.
Because if I wanted to, I could take a pot, fill it with soil, and stick a plant in it. I could
take part of this garden and create a smaller garden somewhere else. I could even take

that smaller garden *inside*, and with proper care, it would still grow. "Potted plant" seems too domesticated a term for miracle.

I spot a bit of green in the upturned soil. It's chickweed, a seed carried by wind and bird, and it's already put down roots in my garden. I dislodge it with the tip of my boot, but I know this is a temporary measure. Kick the plant to the side, but wherever it lands, it will just put its roots down again, as if some force is drawing it toward the earth. I also know that it's just a matter of time before this entire plot erupts with life, whether I plant it or not. In many ways, gardening is a race to see who stakes claim to the soil first—whose plants get to grow and where. Mine or nature's?

Because even though I can't see it, the ground is right now teeming with life and the potential for life. And perhaps the best way to understand the soil under my feet is to think of it as an ecosystem painstakingly designed to support flourishing. It regulates moisture and provides a home for microbes. It filters pollutants and reserves nutrients. And if that's not enough, it literally roots plants to the surface of the earth.

Don't let the ubiquity of dirt fool you. It is a wonder.

Which gives me pause when I think that God, when He wanted to make a creature in His own likeness, stooped down, and took a handful of dirt. I once had someone object to my choice to describe human beings this way because she felt that it devalued us. I thought (but did not say) that she did not understand soil. To be marked as soil is no slight. To be marked as soil is to speak of potential and life and vitality.

This does not mean that all soil is healthy. In fact, the very ground from which we were taken was eventually cursed, so that today, poor soil quality is a primary cause of poor yield, especially if the soil's been mismanaged, abused, or stripped of its biodiversity. This is, after all, the point of the parable that Jesus tells about the farmer whose seed falls on different types of soil.

If soil is hard and compact, like a footpath, a seed cannot penetrate it and is quickly eaten by surrounding wildlife. If soil is stony, a seed might initially sprout, but it won't have sufficient room for its roots. If soil is already full of other plants (like my garden threatens to be), a seed can't get enough nutrients and suffocates. But if a seed finds good soil—the kind that's been carefully tended, that's been prepared, that's had the stones and weeds plucked out—it will bring forth a harvest a hundred times itself.

I continue through our plot, kicking aside clumps of dirt as I do. The earth underneath is darker, owing to the moisture it's holding, while the top layer, already dry, is a lighter, rusty brown. This soil is not refined like that in the raised bed of my herb garden; this is working soil, rugged and gritty. But I also see the bits of eggshell and vegetable scraps that we've composted and worked into it. I remember that we'll add a load of manure and work that in too.

The good news about soil—even poor soil—is that it can be cultivated. You may not be able to control the kind of ground you inherit, but you can control what you do with it. The good news about those who've been made from earth is that we too can be cultivated.

Because there's another story Jesus tells His disciples: A landowner has a fig tree that isn't producing fruit, so he decides to cut it down. "Why should it use up the soil?" he reasons. But a wise servant steps in and says, "Sir, leave it alone for one more year, and I'll dig around it and fertilize it. If it bears fruit next year, fine! If not, then cut it down."[3]

So often we focus on poor quality fruit or lack of yield and throw our hands up in defeat. In reality, the real questions are more fundamental: *Do you want a good crop? Do you want to see the fruit of goodness in your life and in those you love? Do you want to see a harvest of righteousness?*

Don't cut the tree down; cultivate the soil. See what happens.

And I can't help but think of all the ways I've been worked over—how many ways and how many times my heart has been broken open, the weeds stripped out, and the rocks dislodged. I can see how the Father's working His soil like any faithful gardener would. I see how He's tending His bit of earth, how He's cultivating the ground until it's honest and good and ready to receive His Word. And I'm confident that, just as He did in Eden, He will cause even the smallest of gardens to flourish with life.

SCRIPTURE

Genesis 2:7–9; 3:17–19 | Luke 8:4–15; 13:6–9 | Philippians 1:6

III.

"They go out to their work, searching for food.
The wilderness yields food for them and for their children."

JOB 24:5 NKJV

———

WHEN I WAS YOUNG, I was deathly afraid of toadstools for the simple reason that I'd been told they would cause my death.

My grandmother was the first to tell me this, and looking back, I find it odd because I know no child who voluntarily eats mushrooms, let alone ones that grow in the wild. Even still, my grandmother felt compelled to warn me of nature's toxicity and to regularly remind me to not eat toadstools. Of course, the warning existed precisely because she did.

Raised in the mountains, my grandmother spent more time outside than inside, the woods and fields more home to her than her house. She kept a large garden and taught me to plant squash among the corn. In summer, she'd pick blackberries and elderberries, and in fall, she'd gather apples and black walnuts. And every spring, she'd forage the woods for a "mess" of young poke greens or other edibles. Knowing children's propensity to mimic behavior, she made sure to tell me to not eat toadstools.

(What's the difference between a toadstool and a mushroom, you wonder? As I remember it, the difference between a toadstool and a mushroom is that a toadstool would kill you and a mushroom would not. But on further inquiry, the word *toadstool* seems to signify the shape of wild fungus most likely to be toxic. If it looks like a stool that a toad could sit on, don't eat it.)

There's more to it than this, of course, as any naturalist can tell you; but with a little knowledge, a spring forest is a wonderful thing. Long before our cultivated plots come into bloom, or even before we've cultivated them, the forest comes to life with enough vegetation to give you hope—but not so much as to make you forget winter's scarcity. The trees will begin to bud even as the ground beneath them lies blanketed with last season's leaves. They'll crunch under your feet as you walk, but you'll also see bits of green poking through them and clusters of wildflowers here and there. The air will hold a slight chill, but the springs and creeks will run with snow melt. If you crane your head back and look up to the sky, you'll be able to see blue between the bare branches, the leafy canopy still a few weeks off; and if you bend your head down and look to the earth, you'll find the earliest wild edibles: pokeweed, ramps, fiddlehead ferns, wild onions and garlic, dandelions, and if you're lucky enough, morels.

As mushrooms go, morels are something of a celebrity sighting, highly prized by chefs and locals alike. Because they're difficult to cultivate, morels have become a multimillion dollar industry with demand met by harvesting them in the wild. But like other wild mushrooms, they require just the right conditions to emerge. They need damp days and rising temperatures; the soil must be moist and reach 50–52 degrees Fahrenheit. And then, as if overnight, they'll burst from the earth.

But you'll need to watch more than the weather to *find* morels. For this, you'll need to know both how to look for them and how to *see* them. Some morel hunters claim that you can find morels near dead and decaying elm, tulip poplar, and ash trees. Others stake out land to hunt year after year. You'll have to search through underbrush, fallen leaves, and new vegetation. You'll have to be patient and thorough. And if all else fails, you can use a "search image" technique in which you hold a picture of a morel in your mind while scanning the ground for a similar shape.

Still, my grandmother's warning was not without cause. Because the same spring forest that offers up morels and other wild edibles, also offers up plants and fungus that are toxic. To make matters worse, some plants are edible only at certain stages; or some parts of the plant are edible, while other parts of the same plant are not. Some toxic plants even masquerade as edible plants, luring the ignorant and inexperienced. For example, not all young ferns can be eaten, despite their coiling heads. Pokeweed that is too old or improperly prepared can leave you with stomach pain. And a false morel is not the same as the true one, so please don't eat the toadstools.

Here are the stakes: The same ground that is blessed is also cursed. The same ground that gives us plants for food also gives us thorns and thistles. It brings forth both life and death. Eat the right thing, and you will live; eat the wrong thing, and you will die.

Given the dangers associated with the earth, it could be easy to skip foraging altogether. And I suppose in a modern context, we have that luxury. Who would take the risk when you can simply buy food at the grocery store? Because despite the growing interest in foraging, I know that we don't do it for the same reasons my grandmother did or her grandmother or her grandmother before that. Foraging is peasant's work, the gifts of the earth to those who most need it. But I also wonder if we're missing out, if we're missing out on morels and ramps and fiddleheads. I wonder if our search for safety means that we're not searching for goodness.

So what are we to do? In foraging circles, the solution is simple: you learn. You learn what is good and what is bad so you can enjoy the good.

Like many such skills, foraging is primarily passed down from person to person; and in the absence of a grandmother to tell you not to eat the toadstools, you can opt for guided walks, classes, and even books. But mostly, you have to put the time in. You have to learn by doing. Because as any seasoned forager can attest, goodness does not grow in neat clumps or carefully tended rows. It is wild, and you have to work for it. You'll have to go out in the chilly spring rain and tramp for miles. You'll have to keep a keen eye, and even then, you'll likely miss what's right in front of your face. You'll have to admit what you don't know, and in humility and patience, learn from others.

Likewise, the psalmist tells us that the earth is full of the Lord's goodness, and in Philippians 4:8, the apostle Paul invites us to forage for this goodness, neither fully accepting nor rejecting what the world offers. Instead, he invites us to search out "whatever is true, whatever is noble, whatever is right, whatever is pure, whatever is lovely, whatever is admirable." Because if you do—if you're humble enough to learn the difference between life and death, if you seek whatever is excellent and worthy of praise, if you look for it in the underbrush and around trees and hidden in the hillsides, if you take the time and make the effort—you're sure to find it.

And when you do, you'll realize that you've been surrounded by the Lord's goodness all along.

SCRIPTURE

Genesis 1:11–12, 29–30 | Psalm 27:13; 33:5; 136:25; 145:15 | Matthew 6:31–33
Romans 12:2 | 1 Thessalonians 5:21 | Philippians 4:8–9

IV.

"Hope deferred makes the heart sick,
but a longing fulfilled is a tree of life."

PROVERBS 13:12

NOTHING CAN MAKE A GARDENER so nervous as an early bloom. This is how it happens. In late winter, the days lengthen and the temperatures rise. You see the crocuses first, and that's fine because you know that this hearty bulb can survive almost anything. You've seen it covered in snow and ice, radiant. The daffodils push through next, and even though it's only February, you don't panic because it happens like this sometimes. You'll notice stray forsythia starting to bud and maybe even bloom, but forsythia are overachievers, and you've seen stray buds since December, so ready are they to show their color.

But then you see silver tips begin to form on the peach tree, and your heart stops. It's much too early. Maybe it was that warm spell a few weeks ago, or maybe the climate *is* changing like they say. You don't know because who can? But what you do know is that it's far too early for peach trees to bud.

So you watch the trees with a wary eye while other people watch them with delight. To them, early buds are a sign of good things to come, of winter's demise and spring's ascendancy. To them, these buds mean life and fruitfulness, festivals and celebrations. They're caught in the heady romance of it all, but they've never had their heart broken by a peach blossom encased in ice. They've never seen an Alberta Clipper descend like a wolf on the fold, and "the Angel of Death spread his wings on the blast."[4]

Let them have their joy; you've got your anxiety. Because you *know*. You know that buds do not mean blooms any more than blooms mean fruit any more than fruit means harvest. Instead, like anyone with your experience, you pace yourself, curb your enthusiasm, and keep desire in check.

The weather holds, and over the next few weeks, the silver tip becomes green and grows to a half-inch green and then a tight cluster. A few days later, you see the first signs of pink. You watch as the sepals loosen, and delicate petals open, gradually revealing stamen and pistil. Soon the branches are swathed in hundreds of thousands of delicate white blossoms promising abundance. You hear the bees at work collecting nectar and carrying pollen from tree to tree. Butterflies and birds too. You sneeze when you walk underneath the branches, your nostrils filled with the fecundity of life.

So you can't help but see them, and you can't help but smell them. You even find yourself smiling as you turn the corner and drive toward home, so pretty are the peach trees lined up in a row. And for a moment, you wonder if it's possible . . . maybe these early blooms are a gift and not a temptation.

But then you remember that you live in hardiness Zone 7a, as determined by the United States Department of Agriculture, and you remember that the last frost date isn't until mid-April. You remember the cold hard fact that it snowed last May. So while you watch the blossoms, you also watch for cold fronts and unexpected dips and winds from the north. It all depends on the thermometer hung near the window with the white curtains.

It might be fine if you were just a few degrees further south. But you're not, and you know danger lurks even after the petals begin to naturally drop off and the ovule begins to swell. And then, one night, it comes. Just as you knew it would. The mercury drops; the wind blows. The warnings scroll across the screen. You gather up the odd blankets and bits of plastic and do what you can because you know what will happen if you don't.

How does one live in this place between longing and fulfillment? How do you dare to hope when the world is so harsh and cares nothing for your good work? How can you sustain hope in the face of it all? How can you not be chilled until your heart slowly freezes over?

I wonder for myself. Because it's not just buds and blooms. It's the ache of children and our dreams for them; it's the burden of communities and our work invested in them. It's the longing for righteousness and praise to flower in all nations and the obvious fact that they don't.

And if I'm honest, it's far too easy to become a cynic in the name of realism; too easy to give up hope because this is the way it is and what will be will be and the sooner you make peace with reality, the better. But then I think, if we were actually realists, we'd acknowledge that sometimes our justified fears don't materialize. If we were actually realists, we'd know that some years, the blooms come and the killing frosts don't. We'd know that some nights you go to sleep in the certain knowledge that all is lost only to awaken to trees that make it safely through.

And we'd have to confess that some days, hope brings forth fruit as a tree of life, and the harvest is plentiful.

It's not lost on me that the book of Genesis opens with a vision of a tree of life and the book of Revelation closes with one—and that all of redemption is bookended by desperate hope. That even when cold death comes closing in, hope calls us to trust a God who is stronger still. This is the difference, I think, between a wary eye and a closed one—one that watches with caution and one that refuses to watch at all. This is the difference, I think, between hope that is deferred and hope that is lost.

Because in the end, a heart that longs for fruitfulness is also a heart that will work for it. A heart that hopes for goodness will plant and prune and wait and pray. Such a heart is not blind to the realities of life; it just knows no other way to live. And so understanding the stakes, such a heart stakes a claim anyway. Such a heart hopes in God.

SCRIPTURE

Genesis 2:9 | Psalm 39:7 | Proverbs 13:12 | Isaiah 61:11
Hebrews 11:1 | Revelation 22:2

V.

BY NOW, SPRING HAS ESTABLISHED itself, and our fears of an unexpected cold snap are well gone. We're enjoying consistently warm days, and we've started cleaning up the brick terrace that sits off the back by pulling weeds, clearing dead leaves, and filling the pots with annuals. In the coming months, we'll eat outside more than in, and I want to be ready.

Nature has been preparing too. The grapevine that climbs the pergola above the terrace is in full leaf, as is the river birch that sits a few yards away. The beds nearby are flowering as they should, and I struggle to remember how it all happened. I remember when both tree and vine were bare, and I remember the first buds, but so gradual was spring's arrival that I find it hard to pinpoint exactly when it came. *When exactly did I let down my guard and trust it?* I'm still a bit startled when I look up and realize that the season has changed.

Of course, the calendar tells me that spring arrived with the vernal equinox, the precise moment when the earth's tilt and the sun's orbit align and day and night are equalized. Here, in the Northern Hemisphere, this astronomical spring comes the third week of March. And I don't discount this. In fact, some people around here take celestial movements so seriously that they even follow them in their planting. They insist on planting by "the signs," sowing crops in accordance with the moon.

But the heavens are not the only way to reckon the seasons. If I chose, I could also record daily temperatures and divide the calendar into even blocks based on the average. This is a meteorological spring. And were I to mark spring this way, I would know that spring began on March 1 and will last through May and that the frost date for our region falls well within it.

Or I could watch for ecological spring, tracking biological signs of readiness—the softening ground, the first buds, or the spring peepers. I think of the returning robins, those charcoal birds, with their breasts the color of my terrace brick, those harbingers of spring whose return Emily Dickinson dreaded so.[5] Part of the thrush family, North American robins are not like their European counterparts who overwinter in one location. Our robins are nomads who move in search of food. *But how do robins know when to move, I wonder? Who tells them spring has come?*

It seems that they, like me, watch the signs. They follow warming weather along the 37° F isotherm (a band that connects locations of relative daily temperature); simultaneously, this same warming trend prompts the earthworm to migrate from deep below the frost line to the earth's surface. And when the time's right, and with a bit of luck, the robin will arrive just behind a weather system that's left the ground soft and soaked, the mist rising and the earthworms with it.

So there you have it: I know spring by the robin and the robin knows spring by the earthworm and the earthworm knows spring by the warming ground and the ground is warmed by the earth's tilt and the sun's rays. And the calendar does its best to keep up.

But who tells the winter to thaw in the first place? Who says it's time for cold and heat to switch, for winter and summer to exchange places? Because even though I wonder every year exactly *when* spring will come, I never wonder *if* it will come. So perhaps the most mysterious thing about the seasons is not their variability but their constancy. Perhaps the most mysterious thing about them is that they exist at all.

Who could have imagined this? What designer would have said, "I'll set everything in motion with enough rhythm to keep things in place, but then, within this order, I'll introduce variability"? Who would set the sun, moon, and stars in the heavens to give us astronomical signs to guide our days, months, and years only to give us the winds and waters to disrupt those same seasons? Who would make a world that is tilted ever so slightly, just enough off balance that He's needed to balance it?

Think of it, an entire cosmos designed to teach you this one thing: to trust Him and Him alone. An entire cosmos designed to teach you faith.

The writer to the Hebrews describes faith this way: "Now faith is confidence in what we hope for and assurance about what we do not see."[6] And so it is with the seasons. It's only because we have seen past seasons that we believe in future ones; it's only because we have seen certain patterns that we act in certain ways. We plant a seed because we believe it will grow, and we harvest because we believe winter will come. So the seasons teach us to believe in a future we cannot yet see, but the unpredictability of the seasons teaches us to trust the One who will bring it to pass.

Because you know as well as I do that faith does not come easily. You know as well as I do that there are times when everything feels off-kilter, when it feels *unseasonable*. You know that sometimes the earth quakes and the waters rise, and it seems like all of it will come undone and drown us. And it's into these times that the Creator speaks again: "As long as the earth endures, seedtime and harvest, cold and heat, summer and winter, day and night will never cease."[7] And then, over the soaked and sodden earth, He once again sets a sign in the sky to prove it.

Now you can understand why the ancients worshiped God along natural rhythms, why fast and feast days aligned with lunar cycles and celestial patterns and times of rain. Worship attends the earth's seasons, not because the earth is to be worshiped, but because seasons teach us the shape of faith. Order in variety. Stability in chaos. Trust in the unknown. So that by looking to the heavens, we find our feet on an ever-turning earth.

SCRIPTURE

Genesis 1:14–15; 8:15–22 | Psalm 74:17 | Jeremiah 5:24 | Hebrews 11:1

VI.

IT WAS A DILEMMA for the ethicists. The kind of dilemma professors include on philosophy exams about trains and switches and the difficult decisions we must make when death is bearing down. But when you needed them, no ethicists were to be found. When you needed them, the philosophers had left, and my uncles had to face the question alone. A robin had built a nest on the axle of the Ferguson tractor, and the fields needed to be mowed. Worse, still, the nest held four perfectly-formed eggs.

My dad's side of the family is oddly sentimental for as practical as everyone is. A set of aging siblings, they're deeply committed to their family and their land. They tend to make their decisions by consensus, and because their sister won't let them sell trees for timber, they don't. By the time the land had passed into their hands, the original farm had already been parceled up, the buildings sold off. But they remember the land being one, so they tend to act as one. They remember the fields that grew corn, the shed that housed a cow for milk, and the chickens that strutted across the yard. They remember the orchard with pear and apple trees, the grape arbor, the gooseberry bush, and the tall pines that flanked the small house that raised them.

It's mostly the work of upkeep now. They plant flowers and replace the mailbox when needed. One brother lives in the home place and another built a country house about three hundred yards from it. Fields that they once cut for hay, they now cut for respectability. They putter and tend and keep watch over it all.

But what are you supposed to do when a robin nests on the tractor? What are you to do when the other tractor won't start? What are you to do when the grass keeps growing and there's only one sunny day in five?

The dilemma presented itself mid-April, and I only knew about it because I'd come home to be with my dad after my mother experienced a massive heart attack. He rushed her to the hospital, and my siblings and I rushed home, flung far from the family land but drawn back to it by the same forces that kept my dad and his siblings nearby.

We arrived at the hospital aware of everything. My mother had become unresponsive during the attack, and it had taken over thirty minutes to re-establish her pulse. Her organs had been without oxygen for too long. Even if her kidneys, liver, and bowel could recover, there was little way to know how her brain had been affected. Doctors and nurses were maintaining her blood pressure with a chemical cocktail and her breathing by a ventilator. There was nothing more they could do, and eventually it would not be enough. Nature would take its course.

Compassionate staff allowed us to keep watch by her bedside, two at a time. We should, they told us, consider removing life support. They advised us to "think of what your mother would want." The implication was clear: We should prioritize our mother's holistic wellbeing over our own discomfort. We should not let our distress lead us to decisions that would not, in the end, change the natural outcome. We should, instead, think of her comfort and her desires.

And so we did.

The difficulty, though, is that my mother is a complex woman, and determining what she would want is not as straightforward as you might think. A woman of deep faith, she would not be afraid of death. A woman who loved her family, she would also not want us in grief. And a woman of intellect, she would prize her cognitive ability above every other. *If she were stripped of that, what would she want?*

In the end, my uncles made the same decision we did: we both decided to let nature take its course.

And whether it was respectability or a deep sense of responsibility, I don't know, but my uncle finally decided to climb onto his tractor and mow the fields. And whether it was sentimentality or an unshakable hope in possibility, I don't know, but my uncle also decided to not remove the bird's nest. Instead, under a blue, mid-April sky, he rode the hills and cut the corners with a nest full of robin's eggs perched on his axle. He turned the wheel and slowed his pace with a bird's nest under the fender. And then when he had finished, when the grass had been cut, he returned the tractor to its spot next to the other and climbed down. He knew what he had to do, but more importantly, he knew what he did not have to do. At least not yet.

We too knew what we had to do, but more importantly, we knew what we did not have to do. At least not yet. Because, while we could do nothing to change what would come, we chose to do nothing to change what *was*. We would let the dilemma be. We would let the complex be complex and the difficult, difficult. We would not think of

our own discomfort or excuse ourselves from the weight of uncertainty. We would wait and keep watch.

It's funny how often we confuse letting nature take its course with death, as if death were the more real, truer thing than life. To "let nature take its course" always means something brutal, vicious, and unwanted. As if death were the reasonable price of living and not an aberration. But what if letting nature take its course sometimes means leaving room for the God of nature to act? What if letting Him act sometimes means staying our hand and choosing to stay in the uncertainty? What if waiting on God sometimes looks like patience and self-control? What if it looks a lot like keeping watch over land and hospital beds and robin's nests?

To not remove the robin's nest, to not remove life support, did nothing to change what nature would eventually do or not do. Nature would run its course. But it would only run the course that God told it to run. And none of us could make it do otherwise.

So instead of waiting on nature, we chose to wait on God. We would wait on the One who made the universe and who sustains all things by His powerful Word. With all the creatures of the earth and with all that He had made, we would wait on Him.

SCRIPTURE

Psalm 24:1; 40; 104:24–30 | Hebrews 1:2–3

VII.

*"By wisdom the Lord laid the earth's foundations,
by understanding he set the heavens in place."*

PROVERBS 3:19

THE MOTHER ROBIN CAME BACK. After my uncle had done his work and climbed down, the mother robin came back. My mother came back too. After the doctors had done their work and stepped away, my mother came back from the brink. But a mother's return does not mean her offspring's survival, or her own. For days, we sat with the uncertainty, not knowing which course nature would take.

Scientifically speaking, the odds of those eggs hatching were slim. They'd been jostled across acres of field without incubation. And who knew how long it'd been before mother robin found them again? For all we knew, she was a silly bird sitting on a nest of rotting eggs. It would take her several days to figure it out, of course, and until she did, she'd sit there in hope like a fool.

Scientifically speaking, the odds of my mother's full recovery were also slim. She'd suffered a heart attack and had been without oxygen. And who knew how much brain damage she suffered before she stabilized? For all we knew, we were silly people holding out hope against the inevitable. It would take several days to figure it out, of course, but until we did, we'd sit there in hope like a mother bird.

But not knowing what else to do, we continued to keep watch, both over my mother and mother robin.

Compassion now meant that we could not be with her, our desire to watch by her bedside thwarted by a microscopic virus that had brought the entire world to a screeching halt. The risk of transmission being too great, we stayed home. I kept my distance from mother robin too because the first time I came upon her, I scared her, and she flew from her nest. Perhaps she thought I'd come for the tractor again. Eventually, I learned to approach her from the opposite side and drop to my belly behind the left tire. Then I'd drag myself along the earth like an infant learning to crawl, my arms staking claim to a few inches of ground and pulling myself forward bit by bit. This all sounds a bit dramatic now as I write it. I suppose it was even then. But in that moment, it made all the sense in the world. I needed to know how she was doing. I needed to watch and *know* even if there was nothing I could *do*.

It was the same with the phone calls from the hospital an hour away. I found myself in a hundred odd positions, desperate for the smallest bit of information: *How is her white blood cell count? How much oxygen is she on? Had they taken scans for fractured ribs? What is her pulse? How does she rate on the Glasgow Coma scale?* A week ago, I did not know what such answers meant, let alone how to form the questions, but here in this new reality, every bite of information felt like life. I kept all the data in a yellow stenographer's notebook and deemed it my sacred duty to not lose one bit.

I suppose my need to know was rooted in all the things that I couldn't know, in all the questions that couldn't be answered. *Would the eggs hatch? Would my mother survive? Would she return to us whole?* But in these moments, I found that the work of waiting on nature and nature's God could only be endured by the asking and answering of questions.

Those who claim faith can sometimes have an uneasy relationship with questions and an equally uneasy relationship with science. Just as those who claim science can have with faith and the questions it presents. So suspicious are each of the other that we often place them in opposition as if both could not simultaneously exist. And when we do, we end up asking silly questions like, "Does prayer work?" and then proceed to find even sillier ways of proving (scientifically speaking) that it does.

This seems shortsighted to me because science can only describe those things that we *think* we know to be true. And as such, science is also an acknowledgment of how much we do not know, confirming the limits of our mind through the constant cycle of inquiry and testing. (After all, those who already know don't have to ask.) In this respect, science is the distinct purview of ignorant creatures attempting to make sense of themselves and the creation in which they've been placed. It is a God-given work, and we must not reject what we *can* see just because there is so much we cannot.

By the same token, we must not presume that what we *can* see is all that exists. We must not confuse our knowledge for His. We must not forget that He is God of both visible and invisible, that it is He who "put wisdom in the heart and gave the mind understanding"[8] in the first place. We must not forget that it is with His great power, He created; and with His great power, He continues to create, knitting blood vessels back together and caring for addled baby robins.

Because eventually, when nature took its course and the God of nature had His way, my mother came home to us, full of life and whole. And a few days later, when nature had

again taken its course and the God of nature
had again had His way, the robin's eggs hatched,
full of life and whole.

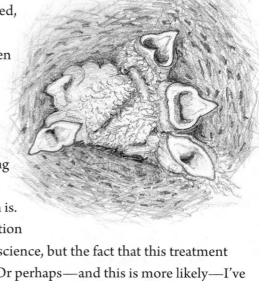

    Now I wonder if the real difference between
what is natural and what is supernatural is
simply our ability to know it. Because if God
is the God of creation, then all of nature is
supernatural. If God is the God of miracles,
then the supernatural is the most natural thing
in the world. And even as I begin to talk this
way, I realize how thin the line between them is.
The fact that a doctor knows the precise titration
of $NaHCO_3$ to save my mother's life may be science, but the fact that this treatment
actually works is nothing short of a miracle. Or perhaps—and this is more likely—I've
been blind to both this whole time. Perhaps I'm the one who's been addled and needs
to be healed. Perhaps I'm the one who must relearn all I thought I knew.

SCRIPTURE

Deuteronomy 29:29 | Job 38 | Proverbs 3:19 | Isaiah 55:8–9
Jeremiah 10:12 | Romans 11:33–36

Summer

I.

———————

THE SUN IS JUST RISING above the trees, and the air is still cool when I step out my kitchen door. I'm barefoot and the grass is wet and cold. Drops of water hang from the clothesline across the yard like so many miniature garments left out to dry, and mist shrouds the mountain in front of the house. Later today, a summer sun will sit high in the sky, blazing hot, and the moisture will burn away, but for now, warmth comes only from the odd sunbeam and the long sleeves of my work shirt.

I've come this morning for the raspberries in the corner patch. It's heavy with them—pink, red, amethyst, and wine—all at various stages of ripening. The canes bend and arc, and morning dew pools on the leaves, cisterns for bird and beetle alike. As I cross the yard, a mourning dove calls for a mate. There's a newness to these mornings, as new as if I were walking in Eden itself, fresh and full of hope. I've come to collect raspberries for breakfast, but more likely, I've come to collect myself.

It's the dew that most makes me think of Eden, how "a mist went up from the earth and watered the whole face of the ground."⁹ Rain is fine for watering, and we're grateful for it, but the dew settles differently somehow. Quiet, steady, and abundant.

Strictly speaking, dew is the result of moisture that condenses as the temperature drops. This cooling happens most often overnight when the sun takes its warming rays to the other side of the earth, which is why we will wake up to dew in the morning—at least when the temperature doesn't drop too far. In late fall and winter, this same moisture might skip the condensation phase entirely and sublimate directly to ice, coating the blades of grass in an exquisite layer of frost. But here on a summer morning, the molecules gather as dew.

By now, *I've* gathered what I need from the thicket, but I find I'm reluctant to leave this moment; this moment when the work of the day is held in check, when I'm not yet asked to produce or perform, when the earth has produced for me. So I wander a bit, over to the garden, past the lilac, toward the apple trees, and the cuffs of my pants soak up the dew with each step.

The book of Exodus tells us that the children of Israel ate manna that came with the dew, that God "rained" it down on them in the wilderness. The people would go to bed without the next day's provision in hand and have to sleep with the hope that it would be there in the morning. I wonder how many of them would lie awake for worry. I would. I do.

Scholars and naturalists wonder whether this dew bread, this "bread of heaven," might have been a product of the tamarisk tree, a desert shrub that leaks a pale sweet sap that crystallizes. Others suggest that it was the secretions of a small, scale insect that feeds on the tamarisk tree through the night. These granules resemble the Scriptural description of manna that was "white like coriander seed and tasted like . . . honey"[10] and could be gathered and made into cakes, as they still are across the Middle East today.

Some may balk at this natural explanation, preferring a more immediately miraculous one. But I wonder, is it any less a miracle that God provides through nature? Is it any less a miracle to feed millions with tamarisk than to feed millions with flocks of quail or water from a rock? Is it any less a miracle to feed one with raspberries gathered among the thorns?

Is it any less a miracle that God's mercies fall like dew every morning? And only in the morning?

Hundreds of years after the manna, a descendent of those desert wanderers writes: "Give me only my daily bread. Otherwise, I may have too much and disown you and say, 'Who is the LORD?' Or I may become poor and steal, and so dishonor the name of my God."[11]

Because here's the paradox of dew and daily bread and mercies that are new every morning: The manna would fall from heaven on every day except the Sabbath, and the people would gather it. But if they tried to accumulate more than a daily portion, it would corrupt. Try to hoard and store up in your barns and rely on yourself and your smarts and your hard work and your foresight, and you'd be a fool. Sure, you might be a rich fool, but you also might not wake to see the next morning's dew.

But too little could corrupt just as easily. Because if you didn't rise to God's morning provision, if you didn't get up and go out and gather, you might find yourself starving in the wilderness, tempted to steal. Instead, the children of Israel had to learn to rely on heaven's *daily* bread just as surely as the disciples learned to pray, "Give us this day . . ."

So too *you* must awaken each day. *You* must walk through the dew. *You* must gather what you have not sown. *You* must return to Him morning by morning for your daily provision. Because make no mistake, it will be provided.

I take a raspberry from my bowl and put it into my mouth. It's still wet, and I taste the dampness before the sweetness. As I roll it around with my tongue, it separates from itself and cleaves naturally along its drupelets. Gradually, the ruby flesh gives way releasing the life-bearing seed hidden in each one. And I pray, "Give us this day our daily bread, and give us this day our dew and mercies, new. Give us this day our raspberries ripe."

SCRIPTURE

Genesis 2:6 | Exodus 16:4 | Numbers 11:7–9 | Proverbs 30:8–9
Lamentations 3:22–23 | Matthew 6:11 | Luke 12:13–21

II.

"Cursed is the ground . . . it will produce thorns and thistles for you,
and you will eat the plants of the field."

GENESIS 3:17—18

I READ AN OBITUARY the other day of a farmer who "raised Angus beef cattle and kept the cleanest hay fields in [the] County. Thistle, chicory, nettles, and multiflora roses were his enemies."[12] And now, you know all you need to know about life outside the Garden. Now you know all you need to know about life east of Eden. We live, we fight the weeds, and then we die.

I think about this as I'm out in the garden, blistering under the summer sun. I should have gotten out here sooner, when it was still low on the horizon and the ground soft with dew. But I delayed, and now, I'm bent over, my face in the dust, sweat trickling down my back. I'm working on the weeds that have grown up between the gaps of the black cloth we laid for the express purpose of preventing weeds. Only a few weeks ago, our garden was neat and spare; today it is teeming with both life and pestilence.

The tomatoes have grown strong, but hornworms as long and as thick as my thumb drag their fat, green bodies along the stems. Cucumber plants have climbed a leaning trellis, but cucumber bugs threaten the very vines that hold them there. White moths dance above the broccoli and cabbage, occasionally dropping down to lay their eggs on them. Eggs that, left unchecked, will hatch into larvae to be discovered in my kitchen. Down at the bottom of the garden, the potatoes are covered in striped, brown beetles, happily feasting on their leaves. And while we haven't had good rain in weeks, somehow the weeds continue to grow—chickweed, henbit, dandelion, plantain, and lamb's quarter. Perhaps we should have planted *them* in the first place.

I grab a handful of foxtail, wrapping my fists around as much of it as I can. I don't wear gloves because I never have; this is how I've always fought the weeds and the world, bare-knuckled and determined. Hunched over, I lower my center of gravity and use my body as a counterweight. It's a tug-of-war, and if my hands slip, they'll burn with a dozen tiny cuts as the blades of grass slice through my skin. (We call them blades for a reason.) I hold tight, willing the clump to loosen, and suddenly with a pop, it does. As the roots come up, I go down and a fine mist of powdery earth sprays into the air, enveloping me in the dust.

It's here in this part of the season that I most feel the words of Genesis:

"Cursed is the ground because of you;
    through painful toil you will eat food from it
    all the days of your life.
It will produce thorns and thistles for you,

and you will eat the plants of the field.
By the sweat of your brow
    you will eat your food
until you return to the ground,
    since from it you were taken;
for dust you are
    and to dust you will return."[13]

And I wonder how long it will be before we just give up. Tending fatigue has already set in, and what seemed manageable back in spring now feels untenable and un-tendable. Soon, we'll find ourselves facing a choice. We can busy ourselves even further, exhausting our efforts, trying to contain the weeds and pests. Or we can let the wheat and tares grow together until harvest; we can accept the fact that our garden will not be pristine. Like the world around us, it will be full of both blessing and curse, both life and death. We can accept that our efforts are not enough.

I already know what we'll choose. We'll choose what we choose every year: We'll choose to give ourselves to the work of harvest and preservation. We'll choose to spend our time staying one step ahead of the curse. And as we pick and freeze green beans and jar tomatoes for soup, we'll know it's the right choice. But we'll still feel shame nonetheless.

If you don't garden, you may not know that such shame exists; but ask any gardener, and he'll tell you. There's a very specific kind of shame that comes from working the earth. The shame of a plot untended or even one that simply *looks* untended. The shame of crops that fail and a field choked by weeds. You feel like it's your fault somehow, that you've done less than you should have. And maybe it's true; maybe you are the sluggard in whose field, "thorns had come up everywhere, the ground [is] covered with weeds."[14]

Maybe if you'd just tried a little harder. Maybe if you hadn't gone on vacation that one weekend. Maybe if you'd just been more diligent from the beginning . . .

I've thought a lot about this kind of shame that plagues gardeners and writers alike. The shame of doing your best and it still not being enough. The shame when your dreams don't produce as you'd hope. The shame of it all being right out there in the open, right out there for every passing soul to see. Your weedy beds and wilted crops. Your wormy peaches and blighted apples.

The shame of not being able to exercise dominion and failing at the one task the man and woman were given to do: to guard and keep the garden.

Not that anyone will say anything. Because while gardeners *will* say to each other, "Your garden looks good this year," they'll never even whisper the opposite. Gardeners are kind, humble souls who know they could be next. *But why, I wonder, why do I feel this shame? Because I can't singlehandedly keep back the curse? Because I can't stop nature from what it will and must do? Because I'm not the Messiah?*

I think of the parable of the tares, how the farmer's field was overrun with weeds, but he let them grow together until the end. I think of how the apostle Paul begged for the thorn to be removed and how the Father simply said, "My grace is sufficient for you, for my power is made perfect in weakness."[15] I think of how Jesus promised that "in this world you will have trouble."[16] And how, just hours later, thorns pressed into His brow and a reed hung from His hand, how the curse mocked His work.

In this world, you will have trouble. In this world, you will eat bread by the sweat of your brow. In this world, you will feel shame and sorrow. In this world, you will wonder whether your work is making any difference at all.

There is no shame in seeing the world for what it is. It is not lack of faith to accept what God Himself says to be true about it. In fact, I wonder if the opposite is so: Does denying the brokenness signal a lack of faith? Do we deny the tares and thistles because we don't believe that He can overcome them? Do we count on our work because we don't trust His?

Then I remember that Jesus also said this: "In this world you will have trouble. But take heart! I have overcome the world."

Take heart! the wheat will grow.

Take heart! the harvest will come.

Take heart! the tares will be gathered up.

Take heart! I am coming to set all things right.

SCRIPTURE

Genesis 2:15; 3:17–19 | Job 31:37–40 | Proverbs 24:30–34 | Isaiah 55:13
Matthew 13:24–29, 36–43 | John 16:33 | 2 Corinthians 12:7–10

III.

"Put on the new self, created to be like God in true righteousness and holiness."

EPHESIANS 4:24

IN WINTER, YOU CAN WALK through the forest and make out every contour of the land. The trees stand like skeletons, their bony limbs fully exposed; the forest floor is open, covered only in last season's decaying leaves. You can trace the rise and fall of the terrain, seeing where boulders protrude and animals have burrowed into the earth to hibernate.

But a summer forest is another thing entirely.

Just weeks after spring's first vegetation emerges, the forest erupts. The leaf canopy and understory grow thick and only the occasional sunbeam breaks through. Closer to the ground, bushes and shrubs hang heavy with foliage and fruit. And on the forest floor, dense herbaceous growth covers the decaying leaves, re-carpeting the woods in green. Along a bustling creek, wildflowers and ferns grow in the soil enriched by seasonal flooding, and I think, yes, this is exactly what a wood should look like in summer.

It's the ferns that most make me think of a summer wood. Quiet and calm, they hint at primeval forests, rich soil, and ancient ways.

I read once that the Victorians were mad for ferns. So much so, they grew them in terrariums, collected and cataloged hundreds of species, and stamped their unique shape on everything from pottery to glass to linen and books. They wrote field guides and organized gathering parties that took them deep into the cool, dark woods in search of new specimens. They called it pteridomania.

And while I don't suffer from this "fern fever," I am fascinated by ferns, fascinated by their order and precision, fascinated by how they display divine purpose and the persistent patterns that undergird all creation. I realize it's asking a lot of a fern to represent cosmic reality, and that's not what I mean to do. But I do think the fern tells us something about how certain patterns repeat themselves, how the simple is complicated and the complicated simple. I do agree with Elizabeth Barrett Browning that "earth's crammed with heaven/And every common bush afire with God."[17]

Channel your inner Victorian for a moment and try this: Take a fern, and lay it flat in front of you. You'll quickly see how it mirrors itself. Split down the middle by a midrib or axis, the blade of the fern is made up of leaflets that branch left and right. These leaflets are called pinna, and they themselves are composed of smaller leaflets of almost the exact same shape. If you look closely, you'll see that each of these pinnules are themselves made of branching and arching shapes that continue the original pattern. Look closely again, and you'll see how pinnule, pinna, blade, and frond are all the same basic shape repeated at both macro and micro levels.

Keep looking and you might begin to lose your head with the dizzying effect of the pattern repeating itself over and over and over again.

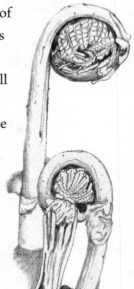

This sameness at all levels is called self-similarity and is related to fractal geometry. And it's all there right from the beginning. When the frond first pushes up through the forest floor in spring, it is coiled tight in a fiddlehead or crozier (shepherd's crook) that protects the tender tips and subdivisions. At this point, they are still small, but through a process called *circinate vernation*, they slowly elongate and harden. The lower leaves open first, providing the necessary photosynthesis for the fern to continue to expand and uncoil.

And so each pinna and pinnule, each leaf and leaflet, emerges in coordination, mirroring the other, dependent on the other, but all in the same pattern as the original.

I think about how much of our own growth is the repetition of patterns, how it happens along a self-similar shape. The Scripture teaches that we welcome strangers and foreigners because God has welcomed us. We rest on the Sabbath day because God rested. And when Jesus teaches us how to love, He tells us to show love in the same way He has shown it to us. We are to forgive as we've been forgiven by God.

I suppose you could say that all of the Christian life could be summed up in the words "as" and "like." "As I have loved you, so you must love one another." ". . . forgiving each other, just as in Christ God forgave you . . ." If we are to mature as we should, it will happen along self-similar patterns, the work of the Spirit slowly uncoiling until the likeness of Christ is reflected throughout the whole of us.

And just as in the fern, this basic shape is both the means and the end, both the goal of growth and the mechanism by which we grow. In his epistle to the Galatians, the apostle Paul explains how our present walk in the Spirit takes shape along a pattern similar to how we began it. He writes, "After beginning by means of the Spirit, are you now trying to finish by means of the flesh?"[18] And again, "Since we live by the Spirit, let us keep in step with the Spirit."[19]

The point is this: there are deep truths that give shape to life with God—truths about grace and repentance, love and sacrifice, life and resurrection. We grow as we continue to uncoil along these same basic patterns, new life supported by old, the lowest leaves emerging first, allowing later ones to grow in the same pattern as the original. If new birth requires humility, confession, and trust, why would new *life* require anything different? And if the grace He bestowed on us was free and abundant, why would we assume that is any less so now? After beginning by the Spirit, why would we finish in the flesh?

No, eternal life unfolds itself in us the same way it began. It began in Christ, and it continues in Christ. This is our *circinate vernation*.

We do not turn in circles, but slowly uncoil and come into life shaped by the person and likeness of God Himself. Until each leaf, each frond, each day, each moment, each relationship, each thought, each word is shaped by His character. Until the whole becomes wholly like Him, majestic and mesmerizing in all His glory.

SCRIPTURE

Luke 10:37 | John 13:34 | 1 Corinthians 11:1 | 2 Corinthians 3:18
Galatians 3:1–14; 5:22–25 | Ephesians 4:24, 32

IV.

I WANDER OUT TO hunt blackberries when the sun is high and a haze hangs across
the field. Everything feels hot and sluggish, and the cows, whose pasture I've invaded,
lift their heads only long enough to acknowledge me and quickly drop them again. The
grass crunches beneath my feet, dry and brittle from lack of rain. In the background,
the high pitched whine of a dog-day cicada rings through the hollows and hills. If I
weren't already perspiring, that sound could make me break out in a Pavlovian sweat,
so much have I associated it with the heat of summer.

Even without seeing it, I can picture it—long and thick with translucent wings
that span almost three inches. This particular cicada is one of the annual
varieties that emerge every summer and live a fairly pedestrian life, at
least for a cicada. It has a black body edged in green, and you can
count on seeing a handful throughout the season. Or maybe,
if you don't see one, you'll find a skincast attached to a tree
or fence post. This memory of the last nymph stage always

makes me think of a ghost, the shell perfectly shaped like a cicada but eerily hollow inside.

But some years—every seventeen to be exact—these annual cicadas are outmatched by a swarm of periodical cicada who synchronize their growth cycles to emerge from the earth *en masse*. That's right, the insects have unionized, and when the ground hits a temperature of 64 degrees, they wake up from a seventeen-year slumber and crawl out of their tunnels through dime-sized holes in the soil.

Grouped by geographic broods, periodical cicada are a natural phenomenon unique to North America, and only those who've experienced it can fully appreciate the scope of what I'm trying to describe. Brood V emerged in southwest Pennsylvania the summer of my sophomore year of college. I was twenty years old, and they were seventeen. I arrived at the beginning of the month, and they arrived at the end. I was one, but if estimates are to be believed, our family's ten acres hosted fifteen million.

I was there. I believe the estimates.

The most common of periodical cicadas is the Pharaoh cicada (*Magicicada septendecim)*, and as its name implies, these insects easily lend themselves to biblical parallels. In fact, when the Pilgrims first encountered a brood in New England, the only context they had to understand their numbers were the plagues that God had sent to free His people from Egypt. And so they called them "locust"—a misnomer that continues to this day, and one that I myself use until my husband, Nathan, corrects me. But unlike the swarms of frogs, lice, and true locust, cicadas are more clumsy than predatory. They'll cover vehicles and trees and fly through the air willy-nilly, searching for any available limb, whether arboreal or human. But for the most part, they are a kind of bounty, a chaotic, unruly abundance that serves a greater purpose.

By emerging together, the cicadas ensure the survival of their species (as well as the survival of many others) through a phenomenon called "predator satiation." The first couple million might become dinner for turtles and raccoons, birds and beasts, but what's a couple million when you've got fifteen to work with? So I don't begrudge them their masses because it guarantees that at least some of them will escape and live long enough to reproduce while also providing a food source for local fauna.

After predators have feasted, the remaining males join together in the recognizable chorus of "weeeeee—whoa" or "phaaaaaa—raoh" and for the next three weeks, the sound of millions of lovesick cicada accompany your every waking act. Stand under a tree whose limbs are filled with them and your ears will fill with their cries. You'll likely end up with a few in your hair as well. Eventually the females will lay eggs in the limbs of thin branches. Then four weeks later, the eggs will hatch and millions of larva will drop from the trees and burrow into the ground to begin their own seventeen year hibernation.

There's another thing here that's biblical in its proportion: time.

What exactly does a cicada do for seventeen years under the ground? In the last seventeen years, I've married, given birth to three children, written books, made mistakes, and have set myself up for more. We're talking nearly two *decades* that these bugs wait in darkness. So what goes on down there in the soil all those years?

The answer is as simple as it is infuriating: growth. What happens hidden in the ground is that the cicada larva grow and mature. For almost two decades, they wait, feeding on the xylem of tree roots until they cycle through five distinct stages of development. For almost two decades, they grow in the darkness so they can emerge in the light.

This reminds me of how oddly God and nature measure time. It also reminds me of how patience and faith are bound up in each other and how we must let patience do her work if we ourselves are to mature. In his second epistle, Peter puts the dilemma this way:

> Scoffers will come, scoffing and following their own evil desires. They will say, "Where is this 'coming' he promised? Ever since our ancestors died, everything goes on as it has since the beginning of creation." . . .
>
> But do not forget this one thing, dear friends: With the Lord a day is like a thousand years, and a thousand years are like a day. The Lord is not slow in keeping his promise, as some understand slowness. Instead he is patient with you, not wanting anyone to perish, but everyone to come to repentance.[20]

By Peter's math, seventeen years is like seventeen thousand and seventeen thousand is like seventeen, and I feel every bit of it. I don't like to think of myself as a scoffer, but I also can't help but think of all the times that God has waited longer than I've wanted Him to.

Why, I wonder, does He wait to rescue his people? Why did He wait so long to hear the Israelites cry under "Phaaaaaa—roah"? Why did He wait so long to send the swarms that would set them free? Why did they sit like cicadas under the earth for four hundred years? And perhaps, more to the point, why does it seem like His timetable and my timetable are so out of sync?

God, it seems, does not measure time only in days and months and years, but also in moments and movements. He is exceedingly long-suffering and waits until "the fullness of time"[21] is come. While we're concerned with *chronos*, He concerns Himself with *kairos*, that moment when everything is in place, when the ground is warm enough and growth is complete. His is a patience good enough and kind enough to give us time to develop in dark, hidden until we can emerge full and complete as one.

SCRIPTURE

Exodus 10:12–20 | Psalm 27:14; 37:7 | Galatians 4:4–7
2 Peter 3:3–9 | James 1:2–4

V.

*"He makes springs pour water into the ravines; it
flows between the mountains."*

PSALM 104:10

MY SON AND I walked to see the Smith's baby goats the other day and ended up playing in the creek that runs through their woods and makes up part of their property line, this side of the water being theirs and the other side being someone else's. It was good to be in the trees, sheltered from the heat. The fields continue to slowly dry and the grass turn brown; and while the clouds hang heavy, they refuse to burst. But here, along the creek, in the shade of the forest, everything continues green, their roots within reach of the water that flows from the earth.

Like most creeks, the Smith's creek starts upstream from a spring that feeds into other springs that grows to a trickle to a stream to a creek. Downstream the Smith's creek will join Back Creek and eventually flow to a rapid rushing river and then on forever to the Atlantic. But from where I stand, it all starts with a spring.

A spring is an unexpected thing, water appearing to come from nowhere, flowing from between rocks or pooling at a low point in the terrain. But a spring doesn't come from nowhere. Beneath the earth lie aquifers, layers of water-permeable rock, gravel, sand, and silt that collect precipitation and store it. We can tap these underground reservoirs by digging wells, but pressure can also force water to the surface through cracks and fissures in the bedrock. The point where groundwater emerges is a spring.

When the Europeans first came to these hills, they scouted out the springs and built beside them. They built homes and barns and, most importantly, spring houses. A small construction, a spring house stands over a spring and is set into the surrounding hillside (as springs often occur at the base of a hillside where the land drops low). It would protect the spring from falling leaves, animal contamination, and other foreign material. Often enclosed in a stone-lined pool, the spring itself would act as a natural refrigerator, maintaining a steady temperature in the spring house throughout the changing seasons. So important were springs that towns and municipalities around here are still known by the springs that first sustained their life.

Because it's not simply that water parches thirst; water makes thirst possible in the first place. Without water, life could not exist. That's why astronomers look for water when they look for signs of extraterrestrial beings. Headlines roar, news flashes: "Water Discovered on Mars!" No other signs of life, yet, but we have found the one thing that makes life possible. We have found the one thing on which all others depend.

Back here on earth, this spring-fed creek is full of life, and we spend time catching it: frogs, newts, water bugs, and unnamed translucent crustaceans. And that's nothing to speak of all the life I can't see, the millions of protozoa and other microorganisms that live in the water as it flows along. I watch a fluorescent orange salamander scurry underneath a rock, and as I lift it, sand and silt churn, immediately clouding the water.

A young voice warns: "Hey! Don't stir the water! I'm trying to catch frogs down here." Lucky frogs.

When I'm at the creek, I understand why it's called *living* water: yes, water supports life, but it is also alive itself, moving and flowing along. I understand why the Scripture says that those who seek God are planted like trees by streams that sustain them even through drought. I understand why John's gospel tells of a woman who came to a spring in the heat of the day, how she came to Jacob's well looking for water and found life.

Jesus says that the life He offers becomes a "spring of water welling up to eternal life."[22] He promises that for the one who believes in Him "rivers of living water will flow from within them."[23] I don't know much about ancient wells, but I do know that a spring doesn't stay at its source. A spring gathers momentum, joins other springs, and together they become a rivulet that becomes a creek that becomes a river that flows to the sea. I know what a watershed is, and I know that the spring must find its way to the ocean.

I think again of the woman who drank that living water and how that spring welled up inside her and life flowed from the ground of her being. I think how water trapped under the earth forces its way through cracks in the rocks, how bubbling streams pour forth from stones. So I'm not at all surprised to read that once her rocky heart split wide open, the water of life poured freely, becoming a stream in the desert, a place for others to drink and live. I'm not at all surprised that this tributary would join other springs, gathering momentum until it was a rushing mighty river flowing to a sea of souls.

I'm not at all surprised that those who drink from the water of life become a source of life themselves.

Thunder rolls overhead, and we decide to head home. We release what we caught and follow the creek as it flows to the road. Perhaps the rain we've prayed for is finally coming. Perhaps the water we've longed for will come down and feed the springs that give us life.

SCRIPTURE

Psalm 1:3; 104:10 | Isaiah 43:19–20 | Jeremiah 17:7–8
John 4:1–30; 7:37–39 | Revelation 22:17

VI.

"All people are like grass, and all their glory is like the flowers of the field."

1 PETER 1:24

I ONCE KNEW AN OLD WOMAN who gathered wildflowers to press between paper towels under heavy sets of books. Once dry, she'd lay them between sheets of tissue paper and seal them with a mixture of white glue and water. The paper would dry crinkled and translucent, the violets, daisies, and buttercups shining through like jewels in stained glass.

By now it's high summer, and the meadows are full grown and grown full of perennial grasses and the clumps of wildflowers that color them. Black-eyed Susan, pale blue chicory, and Queen Anne's lace stand tall and proud, arrayed like Solomon in all his glory. And if I allowed myself the time, I could happily roam the fields, gathering these bits of glory. I'd bring them home and arrange them in pots and press them between paper towels under heavy sets of books. In fact, when I was young and first knew the old woman, that's exactly what I did. That's how I spent my summer days.

But time's the thing, and while God may have a thousand years, I don't.

Today, I find I'm neither young enough nor old enough to spend my days gathering flowers, so I do other work instead. Such things must wait, I think. "Old Time is still a-flying,"[24] and nothing teaches us this as surely as the flowers.

Do not think me cynical for seeing flowers this way; I stand on good authority. In Scripture, both psalmist and prophet speak of our lives as flowers whose days on earth are short. Artists too use flowers as *memento mori,* warning us to remember how quickly death comes. *Vanitas* paintings, particularly popular during the Northern Renaissance, often depicted a flower in various stages of decay within the same still life. Bud, bloom, dying petals—all in one image to remind you that you will die.

Still life, indeed.

I think again of the flower woman who brushed flowers with water and glue. I think of those Dutch and Flemish painters who brushed flowers on canvas with paint. And I can't help but wonder: *If life is so fleeting, why use time this way? If you are old, why spend your last days gathering flowers? If your days are short, why busy yourself with painting?*

To my mind, limited time means limited productivity. If life is short (and it is), you'd better make it count. You'd better get to work. You'd better find a way to do and accomplish and succeed. You'd better toil and spin and provide. And while you do it, you'd better *worry*. You'd better worry about how much you can't get done and how little your work is accomplishing. Because really, it's the least you can do.

But what if the flowers have more to tell us? What if we stopped for just one moment, just long enough to listen to all that they're saying? What if the certainty of death is only half the story?

"Consider how the wild flowers grow," Jesus says on the Galilean hillside. "They do not labor or spin. Yet I tell you, not even Solomon in all his splendor was dressed like one of these. If that is how God clothes the grass of the field, which is here today, and tomorrow is thrown into the fire, how much more will he clothe you—you of little faith!"[25]

So there you have it. After all that worry, after all the warnings about the shortness of our days and the brevity of life, it turns out that God is not a utilitarian. To Him, the length of a life is no measure of its worth; the brevity of a life, no measure of its value. In fact, He understands the vanity of life even better than you do (you who wish only for a hundred years); and knowing it, He cares for you anyway. Or perhaps, He cares for you *because* your life is brief, and He doesn't want you wasting it with worry.

How do I know this? I know because He sprinkles the waysides and hay fields with buttercups and roses. He plants columbine and trillium in the deepest wood.

And He dresses them all—these flowers that have only days to live—in robes finer than the finest kings.

And suddenly you understand His next words: "And do not set your heart on what you will eat or drink; do not worry about it . . . your Father knows that you need them. But seek his kingdom, and these things will be given to you as well. Do not be afraid, little flock, for your Father has been pleased to give you the kingdom."[26]

Because life is fleeting, you must not waste your time worrying about it. Because life is fleeting, you must give yourself to those things that truly matter. Because life is fleeting, you must consider the flowers.

I was a child when I first knew the old woman who gathered wildflowers and pressed them between paper towels under heavy books. I was a young woman, only a year married, when she died, her skin as crinkled and translucent as paper sealed with water and glue. She lived longer than most, but she died all the same. And in lieu of flowers, the people sent money and memorials to charities and churches.

In lieu of flowers? Nothing can take the place of flowers. I understand this now. So I'll ask only this of you: When I die, when my days on this earth end and my "one wild and precious life"[27] is over, send the flowers. Send them fresh and send them pressed. Send them in bouquets and boxes. Send them in garlands and wreaths. Send them wild and abundant. But whatever you do, send the flowers.

And when they come and when they wilt, listen to them, and do as they bid you do: trust your Father who cares for them and who cares for you.

SCRIPTURE

Psalm 103:11–18 | Isaiah 40:6–8 | Matthew 6:28–30 | Luke 12:27–30
James 1:10–11 | 1 Peter 1:23–25

VII.

I SIT CROSS-LEGGED in the driveway as I write this, hoping to capture the sky before the light fades or the neighbors begin to wonder. It's late summer, and the days are already showing signs of shortening; I only have moments to take it all in. The sky is streaking pink as the sun drops lower and lower toward the horizon. Pillars of cloud sit in highlight just over and in front of Roanoke Mountain, our mountain—the one that I can see from my front porch on days that are clear enough and the one that is still there even when they aren't and I can't.

And there just to the right, where the mountain drops off, the same clouds are brushed in rose and gold, singed by the receding sun. My first thought is that it looks like a painting, the colors painstakingly mixed and rendered against the sky. It's a Monet or maybe even a Turner, although we're nowhere near the sea. And my mind begins to suggest all kinds of metaphors for God, the Great Artist, who stretches the sky as His canvas. But almost immediately, I'm struck by the inadequacy of my imagination. *Why should the real, truer thing make me think of the copy? Why should God's handiwork remind me of Monet's and not the other way around?*

But it's getting late; I'm thinking too much and seeing too little. The sun sinks behind the tree line, and I find that my mind is playing tricks, making me believe that the sun is still present even though my eye says otherwise. My confusion is justified. Twilight is a paradox; in these moments, the sky is still filled with light even though the sun sits about six degrees below the horizon. In fact, you may not even realize the sun has set because you're still able to go about your business, cheering a little league team or sitting crisscross applesauce in your driveway trying to write. Over the next twenty to thirty minutes, the sun will continue to drop further below the horizon, degree by degree, but you might not notice until it passes 18 degrees and night officially comes.

I've got time yet before this happens, so I focus my eyes again on the clouds, and it seems to me that they've moved to the southeast ever so slightly. I think they're being carried on a breeze, the breeze that I feel like a breath on the back of my hand. But I can't be sure. I don't trust my senses anymore; they're only human after all. *Are the clouds moving? Or do I simply feel the breeze and assume that they cannot be unaffected? Do I believe what stirs me must also stir them?*

Full of color, the sky is deepening, projecting richer hues of pink, yellow, and blue, while just above the horizon, it seems to burn. This too can be explained by angles and light waves. But you'll also have to know something about how particles in the atmosphere scatter light, a phenomenon called Rayleigh scattering.

Sunlight is actually a spectrum of color that ranges from violet-blue to orange-red. During the day, our eyes detect the light from the blue portion of the spectrum, which is scattered as it passes through an atmosphere full of air, water, and dust particles. Now what happens at sunset is that the angle of the sun changes, lengthening the distance that light must pass through the atmosphere. More time in the atmosphere means more opportunity for the violet-blue portion of the wave to scatter before it reaches your eye. What's left when the light finally reaches you is the distinctly redder portion of the spectrum. I read once that the same beam of sunlight that is making a sunset red here in the mountains of Virginia is simultaneously making the sky blue over Colorado.

But I don't think about this as I watch the rose and vermilion dance together. I've moved from paintings to science to poetry and remember the lines my father taught me as a girl:

Red in the morning, sailor's take warning;
Red at night, sailor's delight . . .

I also remember that Jesus said something similar in Matthew 16:2–3 when the Pharisees and Sadducees pressed Him for a sign from heaven: "When evening comes, you say, 'It will be fair weather, for the sky is red,' and in the morning, 'Today it will be stormy, for the sky is red and overcast.' You know how to interpret the appearance of the sky, but you cannot interpret the signs of the times."[28]

But of course Jesus isn't talking about weather patterns. He's not concerned with whether it will rain tomorrow and whether we should take the boats out or leave the planting for later. Instead, He's talking about our ability to perceive what is right in front of our eyes and how easily we miss the work God is doing in full view. A few chapters earlier, Jesus warns His disciples about those who could be "ever seeing but never perceiving."[29] He warns that just having eyes is not enough because some of us will shut them; some of us will shut our God-given eyes lest we see something that we don't want to see.

This makes sense now, watching the heavens shift so quickly in front of me. I understand how one can miss the works of God on display, how your mind can trick you into thinking the sun is still present when it actually sits below the horizon. I understand how quickly night can come upon you as the light recedes further and further. I understand how you can find yourself in darkness and not even realize it until it happens.

The clouds are silhouetted now, flat against the sky. Again, my mind tells me they should be white, lighter than the sky behind them because only moments ago they were. But my eyes tell me they are blue-gray, ominous and deep. *What is real? And what is the reflection? What is the true light and what is changed as the true light recedes? What am I to believe? My mind or my eyes? Can I trust either?*

It turns out that I need the sun to see. I need the sun to make sense of the world and everything in it. Or as C. S. Lewis puts it, "I believe in Christianity as I believe that the Sun has risen, not only because I see it, but because by it I see everything else."[30]

In a few moments, the clouds will again look white—not because the sun has risen but because it has finally fully set. In the darkness, the clouds will contrast against a black sky. Light from the sun will radiate over 93 million miles across the galaxy to bounce from the moon, reflect off it, and finally hit my eye as cool white. So that even in the darkness, even in the night, I am not left without the light.

Even in the night, the heavens still declare His greatness. Even in the night, eyes that are open to His glory can see.

SCRIPTURE

Psalm 19:1–6 | Job 37:14–24 | Matthew 13:10–17; 16:1–4

Fall

I.

"Honor the Lᴏʀᴅ with your wealth, with the firstfruits of all your crops; then your barns will be filled to overflowing, and your vats will brim over with new wine."

PROVERBS 3:9—10

———————————

FOR THE LAST FEW WEEKS, we've been busy gathering in, the work of the season shifting from tending the earth to harvesting what it's produced. Despite our best efforts, though, we can't keep up. Tomatoes sit in rows waiting to be processed and beans in buckets. Figs ripen on the tree while apples drop. Soon we'll gather the harder squashes, pumpkin and butternut, whose skins needed the extra time to thicken. And if we want, we could put in another set of cold crops—broccoli, cabbage, Brussels sprouts, and kale. We freeze and can and dry and give away, but the harvest is more than we can handle.

The woods have come into harvest too. Squirrels and chipmunks gather their winter stores of seeds and acorns, and the black walnuts have begun to fall, their yellow-green outer husks already blackened with age. We prefer the bold, earthier flavor of black walnuts to orchard-grown English walnuts, and this winter, we'll make black walnut cakes and banana black walnut pancakes. But first we'll have to collect them, slip off their inky outer husks, and let them cure. Eventually we'll shell them, picking out the meat, bit by mouth-watering bit.

The harvest season is always generous if not unpredictable. We plant the same slate of crops every year; and every year, the woods produce nuts, berries, and seeds. But you'll never know exactly what you'll harvest until the end because you never know what will grow best. Variations in temperature, rain, and light all combine to create unique growing seasons that benefit certain crops and hinder others. Have a wet, hot summer, and your blackberries will be plump and ripe by early July. But that same dampness also facilitates the growth of rust, and you might find your apple trees covered in fungus.

In spite of the unpredictability of harvest, or maybe because of it, you plant anyway, faithfully tending and surrendering yourself to nature's whims. Besides, if you pay too much attention, you'll be paralyzed. Try to get it just right, and you'll end up getting nothing. "Whoever watches the wind will not plant; whoever looks at the clouds will not reap," the preacher writes in Ecclesiastes. "As you do not know the path of the wind . . . so you cannot understand the work of God, the Maker of all things. Sow your seed in the morning, and at evening let your hands not be idle, for you do not know which will succeed, whether this or that, or whether both will do equally well."[31]

Only at harvest can you know what your labors have brought forth. Only then will you know that it was a good year for peaches and a bad one for cucumbers. Nature's a good storyteller in this respect, holding you in suspense until the final chapter. Maybe that's why, despite the uncertainty, I always enjoy watching the growing season play out; I always enjoy discovering the unique shape of a year.

But if I'm honest (and I try to be), I know that my ability to delight in this seasonal drama is rooted in abundance. My life and the lives of those I love do not depend exclusively on the work of my hands. Or the whim of a growing season. If a certain crop does well, all the better, but if it does poorly, I can purchase food elsewhere. There was a time, perhaps, when I would have felt guilty about this. There was a time too when I believed that self-sufficiency was the goal—that being a "real" gardener meant taking care of yourself and not relying on others.

But in speaking of the harvest of the kingdom, Jesus reminds His disciples that the saying "'one sows and another reaps' is true. I sent you to reap what you have not worked for. Others have done the hard work, and you have reaped the benefits of their labor."[32] And so, in God's providence, harvest is meant to be a time of interdependence and communion, simultaneously abundant and limited. Self-sufficiency was never the goal. Relying exclusively on your own work was never the end. Because as much as harvest teaches you to make peace with the unpredictable, it also teaches you to make peace with others and live in mutuality. All so the sower and reaper can rejoice together.

This mutuality and generosity lies beneath the Old Testament command to not harvest the corners of fields. During the time of gathering in, the Israelites were to leave some of their crops for the needy—the widow, the orphan, the stranger. The first fruits belonged to God, and the last fruits belonged to their neighbors. Because more than anyone, gardeners know that the harvest is unpredictable; gardeners know that you can work and do your best, and the elements can still turn against you. More than anyone, those who work the fields know how quickly life can change, how quickly you yourself could be needy. And so, more than anyone, they know that the wild abundance of harvest is to be shared.

Today, I'm grateful to live in a space between subsistence and decadence, between scarcity and consumption. It feels like a gift. I can work for harvest, enjoying the fruit of my labor, while also knowing that my work was never going to be enough anyway. I can give tomatoes away, and I can leave a few on the vine without fear. And I wonder if this is what it means to flourish, to exist in a place where limits are no liability because abundance is sure. I wonder if this is Eden.

Grace to work. Grace to receive. Grace to know it never depended on me in the first place.

SCRIPTURE

Leviticus 23:22 | Deuteronomy 24:19 | Proverbs 3:9–10
Ecclesiastes 11:4–6 | John 4:34–38 | 1 Corinthians 1:3–9; 9:9–11
2 Corinthians 9:6–10

II.

LIKE SPRING, AUTUMN COMES in gradually, and those things that we most associate with it—cooling temperatures and blue skies over browning fields—do as well. With the heat of high summer past, we bring out our long-sleeved shirts and sweaters and kindle fires. If spring is the sunrise of the year, autumn is sunset, the gathering dusk before winter's night. And just as the sun descends in a blaze of burning glory, autumn is determined to do the same, coloring the hills in burnished gold and leaving us gaping in wonder.

The mountains here in southwest Virginia are home to over a hundred species of trees. Technically defined as a temperate broadleaf and mixed forest, the abundance of deciduous trees (those trees that shed their leaves each season) also means that come mid-autumn, these hills burst into color in the reverse of how they originally budded. While spring works its way up the mountains, autumn works its way down with the trees at the highest elevations coloring first. Yellow beeches, crimson dogwoods, gold-bronze hickories, rusty oaks, and the simple majesty of the brilliant scarlet maples.

Accented by the deep green of Virginia pines, hemlocks, and cedars, it's no wonder
that people drive from hours away to see our hills robed in joy.
So significant is this annual show that scientists have
developed finely calibrated algorithms to predict when color
will peak each year. And those regions that rely on tourist
dollars find themselves also relying on a host of data points and
meteorological factors to know when to expect visitors. Local
media will announce the weekends like a coming snow storm;
instead of inches and icy conditions, they'll predict peak days
and exactly how brilliant we can expect the show to be. But like so many things
in this world, you never know until it actually happens, and you never know whether
you've peaked until after you do.

Still, it's not altogether a mystery. As autumn comes and the earth tilts away from
the sun, the days shorten and temperatures drop, sending green plants and tree leaves
into senescence, the gradual deterioration process that accompanies aging. Less
daylight means the production of chlorophyll slows, which in turn initiates chemical
reactions and allows the pigments underneath the green—yellow, orange, brown, and
red—to dominate. Eventually photosynthesis halts altogether. The death of the leaf is
certain now as cellular respiration ends, but just as certain is the fiery show before it
falls to the earth to die.

That's the facts of it anyway. But anyone who's seen an autumn hillside knows
that facts are just the beginning. After all, if the heavens declare the glory of God, if
October blue skies and billowy white clouds tell forth His praise, what does it mean
that the trees of the wood burst into song just before winter silences them? What does

it mean that anthocyanins turn the maples red and carotenoids turn the sassafras yellow and together they paint the oaks and sycamores brown? What does it mean that the leaves summon their last breath for one last burst of charismatic praise and Pentecostal abandon?

And what does it mean that I can't help but stop and stare?

The poets and prophets speak of trees that celebrate, trees that dance and sing and clap their hands before the Lord. They speak of trees that raise their voice and raise their limbs to the One who's coming to set all things right. This is a strange thing and one I wouldn't believe except for the facts: Leaves are loudest just before they die. "Hear, hear!" they shout. "Pay attention to what I need to say!" And according to the psalmist, this is what they have to say:

> Let all the trees of the forest sing for joy.
> Let all creation rejoice before the LORD, for he comes,
>   he comes to judge the earth.
> He will judge the world in righteousness
>   and the peoples in his faithfulness.[33]

And now you understand why a dying creation would long to proclaim this message. Now you understand why it's essential that, in their death, the leaves proclaim the King of life. Because if there's one thing they must tell you, if there's one thing we must hear, it's that the Lord of Creation is coming to set all things right.

In Romans 8, the apostle Paul makes a strange statement: he writes that creation understands that the world is not as it should be, that it has been subjected to decay, that it "groans" with us, waiting for righteousness and redemption to reign. He writes that, just like us, it waits in hope. And a creation that can groan in hope is a creation that can praise. Trees that long for righteousness are trees that can spend their dying breath praising the One who will one day deliver them.

And then I wonder, *Is it really so strange after all?* Is it so strange that the God who does not live in shrines made by human hands would be worshiped by the woods and trees and mountains that He has made? Is it so strange that the God who gives everyone and everything breath would be worshiped with that same breath, even a dying one? Is it so strange that the last words of the leaves are "Hosanna! Blessed is He who comes in the name of the LORD"?

Is it so strange that this would be on our dying lips as well?

SCRIPTURE

1 Chronicles 16:33 | Psalm 65:12; 96:12–13 | Isaiah 44:23; 55:12
Luke 19:39–40 | Acts 17:24–25 | Romans 1:19–20; 8:19–25

III.

"But let justice roll down like waters, and righteousness like an ever-flowing stream."

AMOS 5:24 ESV

———————————————————

IT'D BEEN RAINING HARD ALL MORNING when I got the call. By mid-October, we'd had a wet fall, making up for summer's dryness; the ground was thoroughly soaked when the remnants of a hurricane came through. We knew it was coming and had been watching the weather all week. We checked our basement to make sure the sump pumps were in good working order. (One fall they were not, and as I sat at my desk writing, I nearly floated away.) We bought water absorbing jams to put under the door and pulled out a stock of old towels to soak up the water that would find its way in regardless. Then we sent the kids off to school under chilly, gray skies, hoping for the best.

The call came shortly after one o'clock: "Come get your children. Now."

People around here talk about the flood of '85, how quickly it swept down the hills and flooded the town that sits in the bottom. That's the problem with being ringed by mountains; all the water from all the springs from all the streams from all the creeks from all the rivers flow down, down, down to the lowest point. They gather momentum and gather in the waterways below. They overflow their banks and plow through whatever lies in their path. A muddy, rushing effusion.

I grab my keys and jacket and head out. I don't know if my tires are right for this weather, but they're the tires I have, so they're the tires that will have to do. Heavy drops of rain fall on my windshield, and the wipers struggle to keep up. Along the road, ditches and gullies channel the water into temporary streams. The road that runs along the river and past the grocery store will flood; there's no doubt of that. I just wonder whether I can get down and back before it does. The water is inching closer to the road, and by the time I drive the twenty minutes to the next town, it will be covered.

It's chaos at the school—parents, teachers, and students all jumbled together, all sharing what they've seen and where the water's high. I stand outside in the rain waiting for my kids and keeping a close eye on the time. Each drop that falls will become part of that rushing torrent I'm trying to outrun. Finally, they emerge and we make our way home. The Parkway is closed; uprooted trees lie across the road. So I head back through town, navigating the streets as water rushes toward the storm drains. We cross the bridge by the old silk mill while the river churns beneath. A few detours later, we arrive at home. We're safe, and the basement's still dry. But by late afternoon, the fire department is rescuing people near Back Creek with high water boats. I see a picture where a road once stood but now a river flows; the road sign is just visible above the water line.

And then as quickly as it came, it leaves. The waters recede. The force and flood abate. Like a flash of lightning, it strikes and is gone. It will take weeks, months, years to understand what just happened.

Large trees are down everywhere, their root systems helpless when the earth beneath them moves. Roads too are washed away, and pieces of asphalt lie in farmers' fields. I have a friend who had both a low water bridge and a high water bridge on her property. Today she has none. The hillside behind an elderly woman's house now sits in her backyard just inches from her door. It will take two years to remove it because no one can decide whose dirt it is once it slips past the property line. Does the hill belong to the one who built on the top of it or to the one who built at the bottom?

And just down the road, a pond broke. I don't know the name of it or whether it even has a name. I do know it sits in a dip in the land and that I drive past it several times a week. A green heron lives there and so do the spring peepers that he eats. It was ringed by cattails and brushes and had a small dock. It was a landmark. And now it isn't.

The pond of philosopher-farmer Wendell Berry ruptured after a similarly wet fall, and he took it as proof of his own hubris, that despite his best intentions, he'd damaged the world around him. "The trouble was the familiar one," he writes, "too much power, too little knowledge. The fault was mine."[34] And perhaps he's right. All the same, I don't agree entirely with Berry here. There's no stopping a flood, and that's exactly the point. The rain comes down on the just and unjust, and we're all swept away by its power. If there's kind of hubris to cut a pond into the earth, there's another kind of hubris that doesn't think the earth will do exactly what it wants with it. When the waters come, they rearrange the world to their own liking.

Knowing this about floods, it makes sense that the Scripture uses floods to picture God's judgment. You know of Noah's flood, how God grieved the wickedness that filled the earth and how He sent forty days of rain down. Perhaps you know too how the prophet Isaiah proclaimed the Lord's judgment would be like "mighty floodwaters"—

"It will overflow all its channels,
    run over all its banks
and sweep on into Judah, swirling over it,
    passing through it and reaching up to the neck.
Its outspread wings will cover the breadth of your land,
    Immanuel!"[35]

When God's judgment comes, it is unstoppable. The waters wash over everything in their path, tearing earth from root and home from foundation. And yet, some survive. Noah is preserved and the remnant of Israel saved. And I wonder, *What's the difference? Why is one kept safe and another lost? Why does one house stand and another collapse?*

Rain from heaven may fall on both the just and the unjust, but only the just prepare for it. Because as much as the Scripture speaks of God's judgment as a mighty flood, it uses the same language to describe His justice. To put a finer point on it, God's judgment is His justice working itself out, setting the world right. So that like a flood, when God's justice comes rolling down His holy mountain, it rearranges and reshapes the earth below.

To the unjust, God's justice feels like destruction because it eradicates everything they've built unjustly. It sweeps away all they'd hoped for and in. But to those who humble themselves, who confess their sins, who align themselves with God's ways even now; to those who as Jesus says "hears these words of mine and puts them into practice," justice feels like righteousness and a mighty stream. The rain may fall and the rivers rise and the winds blow, but the house stands firm.

When we pray, "Your kingdom come, your will be done, on earth as it is in heaven," we're praying with Amos for the Lord of justice to call "for the waters . . . and pour them out over the face of the land."[36] We're praying for God's justice to roll down the mountain and flood our land. But because His justice also means His judgment, we immediately beg the Father to "forgive us our debts, as we also have forgiven our debtors."

Because those who long for God's justice also know that they will only endure by His mercy. Those who pray for God's coming kingdom know that it will be the ruin of theirs. Those who long for earth to be like heaven know that they must be the first to move in that direction. So that with the psalmist, those who long for justice learn to quickly acknowledge their own sin and wait on the Lord's forgiveness.

And thus, battened down, we cry out for the flood of God's justice to come rolling down; we cry out for it to come and reshape and reform our world. And as we cry, we trust that when the waters come, He will be with us as we pass through them. And thus, trusting, we find Him our hiding place and ark in the storm.

SCRIPTURE

Genesis 6:11–21 | Psalm 29:3–4; 32:5–7; 93:3–4 | Isaiah 8:6–8; 43:1–2
Amos 5:8–9, 24 | Matthew 7:24–29; 24:36–40 | Luke 6:46–49

IV.

"Does the hawk take flight by your wisdom and spread
its wings toward the south?"

JOB 39:26

WE HEADED UP INTO the mountains today to hike part of Rock Castle Gorge. It will be cooler up there, the change in only a couple thousand feet bringing lower temperatures and clearer skies. But after the last few weeks, it's a cool dryness we welcome. We dress in layers, but we'll likely shed some of them along the way.

We're only doing the highest part of the trail, the part that runs along Rocky Knob and loops back on itself. It's all we have time for, but someday soon, Nathan tells me, we'll do the whole eleven miles that drop down to Rock Castle and Little Rock Castle Creeks. Today, though, we focus on the ridge.

The trail itself is only moderately difficult, but it's also only a couple feet wide at some points that also happen to be the highest ones. So while you're not exactly taking your life in your hands, you certainly feel like it, walking as you are on the edge of the earth. This high, the trees are short and irregular, bent by the winds that blow over them and eventually drop on the leeward side of the ridge. The sky is closer than it's ever been, and hawks soar just yards away from us.

It's a strange thing to be eye-level with a hawk, the mountains having lifted me and the winds lifting her. She seems to fly effortlessly, without even moving her wings, simply riding the warm air as it rises. So confident and powerful is her flight that, for a moment, I'm tempted to join her, to test the strength of the air that holds her aloft. I resist, consciously reminding myself that I can't just step off the edge and fly. But I want to.

Throughout the day, we see only a handful of hawks, and Nathan tells me that they're probably stragglers finally making their journey south. Had we come a few weeks earlier, we might have seen hundreds, thousands even, gathering and kettling on these updrafts and thermals. Broad-winged, red-tailed, and red-shouldered hawks making up the bulk of them, we might have also seen the smaller Cooper's hawk along with eagles, kestrels, and vultures.

Bird migration is mostly a question of moving to find food when sources become scarce. So the hawks I see today are likely headed to Central and South America along the back of the Appalachians and around the Gulf following "leading lines" or topographical features that guide and funnel birds along a certain path. Our mountains make particularly good leading lines and act as a kind of superhighway all along the East Coast, their ridges naturally deflecting and creating the air currents the hawks ride south. Once there, they'll feast for a few months until they eventually take a similar route back in spring.

Ornithologists have learned a lot about migration—when and why and, to some degree, how—but they still don't know exactly what tells a hawk to migrate or how they know where and when to go. But this much is sure: Hawks know. And each fall, they ride the currents south, and each spring, they ride them back north again.

In Jeremiah 8, the prophet speaks of bird migration and wonders how birds can be so smart and God's people so foolish: "Even the stork in the sky knows her appointed seasons," he says, "and the dove, the swift and the thrust observe the time of their migration. But my people do not know the requirements of the LORD."[37] And it's true. Birds know where and when to come and return. They don't wander off and become lost like we do. They follow the mountains and landmarks and invisible passageways in the wind. They know just how to turn their wing and catch the air and let it carry them.

And maybe this is the point. It's not that hawks know something we don't. It's not that hawks are more intelligent than we are. It's that hawks know how to submit to a power higher than themselves. After all, when it comes to a hawk's migration, the wind does most of the work.

Because of the laws of aerodynamics, a hawk can travel tens and even hundreds of miles on just a few wingbeats. So not only do the winds carry hawks where they need to go, guiding them to provision and rest, they also preserve their energy along the route. And unlike us, hawks are wise enough to submit to them. Instead of willfully and arrogantly pursuing their own way, instead of fighting the wind, hawks lean into and acknowledge it and let it carry them.

No, the problem isn't that we're not intelligent; it's that we're arrogant. We are not humble enough to submit to the One higher than us. Instead, as Jeremiah puts it, each "pursues their own course . . . [and] have rejected the word of the Lord." We lean on our own understanding and insist on our own way. We resist the very thing that will carry us along.

Perhaps, then, this is what Isaiah means about those who learn to wait and hope in the Lord. Perhaps this is how they renew their strength and soar on their wings. Instead of fighting against the ways of the Lord, they learn to lean into and acknowledge them and let it take them where they need to go.

And perhaps this is why David asks the Lord to lead him in His righteousness and why we ask Him to "lead us not into temptation, but deliver us from evil." Just as the winds and mountains guide the hawk safely to provision and rest, the ways of the Lord guide us to the same. So that in learning to trust Him with all our heart and to acknowledge Him in all our ways, our path will be made straight before us. In learning to let Him lead, we will find our way.

SCRIPTURE

Job 39:26 | Psalm 24:4–5 | Proverbs 3:5–6 | Jeremiah 8:6–8
Isaiah 40:31 | Matthew 6:13

V.

"Out of the south comes the storm, and out of the north the cold.
From the breath of God ice is made, and the expanse of the waters is frozen."

JOB 37:9—10 NASB

I WAITED TOO LONG. I waited too long, and now the killing frost has come. After weeks of wet weather, we had a break of mild, sunny days—the kind that make the leaves brilliant and make you want to hike the ridges and hills. Evening temperatures dipped, but it was still warm enough for my herbs to continue in their raised beds. They'd done really well this year and were still thick and abundant into October, with even the basil still growing strong. I'd already harvested a significant crop in the middle of summer, processing it with olive oil and freezing it into cubes for cooking later this winter. I meant to take one final cutting that would equal my earlier one, but the killing frost took it instead.

Around here, you can expect a hard or killing frost mid- to late-October. Some years, like this one, you'll get a reprieve and enjoy a few extra weeks of warm weather. But you're living on borrowed time and death stalks. So when I awoke this morning and found the lawn covered in ice crystals, glinting frost, I knew I'd waited too long.

I can see my breath as I step out of the house, the air from my lungs condensing and crystallizing in the cold. Because the human body is almost seventy percent water, our breath is saturated with moisture; when it exits the body at around ninety-eight degrees Fahrenheit and hits cold air, it quickly cools, making it unable to hold as much water. The tiny droplets condense and fall out of the air, creating the misty vapor we see in front of our faces. A similar thing happens to create frost. As temperatures drop overnight and the air cools, water vapor condenses and sublimates onto surrounding objects, patio chairs, pots, vehicles, trees, and plants, coating them in a layer of delicate ice crystals.

This morning, it's still cold enough to see my breath, but it's not so cold that I need more than a warm coat. That's half the tragedy of a killing frost after all. Temperatures may drop below freezing during the night, but by morning, the sun will come up and by noon, temperatures will be well above freezing. Ice crystals will melt off the grass and windows, and the day will be pleasant. But the damage is already done. It only takes a few hours of freezing in the middle of the night to bring an end to life.

I rub my hands together and blow through them, seeing my breath again. Then I shove them in my pockets and begin to inspect the frost's work. With the sun up, the ice on the grass is already melting and only that in shadow remains. A few stray maple leaves hang edged in ice, and the grapevine that climbs over the terrace droops brown and curled. The last of the potted flowers on the terrace were hit as well. Reluctantly, I stray over to where the herbs sit, but even from yards away, I can see that the basil is gone. The hardier plants are just tinged, but the entire architecture of the basil has changed. Yesterday it was a bush, leafy and green; this morning, the leaves hang brown and limp against the stalks.

Some plants might be able to survive a light frost that settles on their leaves, especially if they sit near a building or under another plant or shrub that creates a microclimate. But the real danger comes from within. Because plant cells are filled with water, they freeze when the temperature drops low enough and stays low enough, long enough; and because water expands when it freezes, tiny shards of ice cut through the cell wall, rupturing and damaging the soft tissue. The plant turns to ice from the inside out.

When I see my basil, I know exactly what happened; and I know there's no repairing the damage. I'm not shocked, but I can't help but feel a little disappointed. This is officially the end. There's a point when everything is growing and then it's not. There's a point when the frost comes, and the only thing you can do is try to get out of its way. This is why we make calendars and predictions. This is why we watch the weather. Because we can't control it; we must prepare ourselves for it. We must cut our basil in time.

When I think of how powerful frost is, how it can change life to death, it makes sense that the Scripture speaks of frost as the breath of God, linking it closely to both His power and His Word. "He sends his command to the earth," the psalmist writes. "He spreads the snow like wool and scatters the frost like ashes. He hurls down his hail like pebbles. Who can withstand his icy blast?"[38]

It's a good question. *Who can stand before His icy blast? Which one of us can hold back the frost? Who among us can stop what the Almighty will do?* It was with His breath, after all, that He spoke the words that formed the earth. It was with His breath that He gave life to those who bear His image. It was with His breath that He makes them alive once more. All He has to do is breathe, and things happen. All He has to do is do the most natural thing in the world.

And suddenly, I understand why the writer of Hebrews pleads with us to heed the Holy Spirit, to heed the Breath of God, calling to us to humble ourselves before Him while it is still *today*. Suddenly I understand the risk of waiting. I understand the risk of rejecting the Word of God and hardening yourself in unbelief. I realize that you can freeze from the inside out and rupture yourself beyond repair. Wait too long, and you'll die from a cold, hard heart.

But there's mercy here too because it is also the Holy Spirit—the Breath of God—who calls us, warns us, and softens us. The same God whose breath brings the frost is the same God whose breath thaws it. "He sends his word and melts them," the psalmist continues. "He stirs up his breezes, and the waters flow."[39]

And so we also find the answer to the psalmist's question, "Who can withstand His icy blast?" No one but the Lord Himself. No one but the One who made the cold in the first place. The One who sends the frost is the One who can make it leave. The One who judges is the One who pardons. The One who condemns is the One who saves. And it is on His mercy we depend.

SCRIPTURE

Job 33:4; 37:10; 38:29–30 | Psalm 78:47; 147:15–18
2 Corinthians 6:1–2 | Hebrews 3:7–8, 12–15

VI.

*"As the deer longs for flowing streams, so I long for you, God.
I thirst for God, the living God."*

PSALM 42:1—2 CSB

THERE'S A ROAD I TAKE almost every day that dips and curves down to town. It's barely wide enough for two vehicles to pass, and the grade is steep—too steep for the school buses and delivery trucks that insist on using it. But it's the shortest distance between two points, and so I, and everyone else, insist on using it too. Even on icy mornings like today. The road starts at the top of a hill with too tight a turn, and if you try to take it while another vehicle is coming from the opposite direction, you'll find yourself in a game of chicken. One of you will have to wait. It's the same when you meet a school bus going up and down; except in that case, you know you'll be the one to wait, come to a full stop, and pull off onto the grassy shoulder.

To make matters more interesting, the local white-tailed deer (*Odocoileus virginianus*) are determined that their path must also cross this road, right in the middle of the steepest part.

One of the first things you learn in navigating country roads is that white-tailed deer have their own paths. They have an entire network of unmarked highways and byways that transverse the countryside, cutting across fields, through forests, and over Randall Road. And they seem to have little concern for whomever else might be using it. I've seen many negligent doe grazing beside the road with a pair of spotted fawns only to lead them straight across the asphalt completely oblivious to the danger posed by oncoming vehicles. Other times it might be a majestic buck who'll leap and bound with just enough time to make it through another season with his points intact. We have as fine a network of roads as anyone in the commonwealth of Virginia, but these four-legged ingrates refuse to acknowledge them. My ways are not your ways says the Lord and the white-tailed deer.

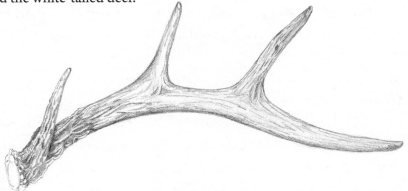

So you learn to look out for deer because when bone and metal and flesh and fiberglass collide, there are no winners. As many times as I've seen a deer escape certain death, I've also seen them die. I've seen their rotting carcasses beside the road and in the middle of it. I've seen their necks wrenched, bent in a most unnatural fashion, their tongues lolling. I've seen the mangled vehicles and broken windshields. So I also wonder, *Why don't these deer seem to care to look out for us? Why do they insist*

on following their own way even when it endangers them? Exactly how long have they been keeping to these ancient paths? And how long have these paths been keeping them?

One such path runs diagonally across our land until it intersects the road. Deer will emerge from the wood and walk, fully exposed, through the back field, along the garden plot, and through our yard. In one respect, I understand their confidence. They've learned by experience that we cannot hunt this close to the house, so they take full advantage of it. But in another, I'm always amazed by the certainty with which they follow their route. It is straight and predictable, and they never stray from it. When the snow lies on the ground, I'll look up from my kitchen window and see a line of prints across the yard and know precisely how they were formed. Even when the earth is blanketed in white, these deer follow the path exactly, as if some invisible force were drawing them along.

To be fair, these deer paths existed long before we interrupted them with our houses and highways. More than simply creatures of habit, deer are creatures of memory and need, driven by elemental desire to find the shortest, safest distance between bedding area, grazing land, and water source. Hunger, thirst, rest, and safety combine to funnel them along certain routes, and over time these routes become established. As mothers raise their young along these same paths, they learn them well, and so it continues. Fittingly, a track that has been trampled by enough use is called a *desire path*. It's the path that will take you to your desire, and soon enough you'll know it by heart.

In Psalm 42, the psalmist likens his desire for God to a deer's longing for a water source. Older translations have rendered the first line of the psalm as "as the hart panteth," but this can be confusing to modern readers. The image is not of a deer overcome by fatigue, thirsting for a drink to quench the fire in his lungs, so much as that of a deer steadily, persistently following his longing to water. Less about desperation, it's more about how desire and habits drive us in predictable ways. So that when the psalmist speaks of his longing for God, he's describing a longing as basic and as formative as thirst and hunger; he's describing the kind of longings that drive deer along the back of my field and across Randall Road.

And suddenly we realize that we too are creatures of habit and memory. We realize how certain paths have been passed down to us and how we lead our young down those same paths. We realize the significance of teaching them to desire rightly, to love the Lord their God with all their heart, with all their soul, and with all their strength. And so we talk about them when we're bedding down and when we're rising up and when we're walking along the road. So that in leading them down the same path over and over and over again, together we find our way. We find our way to the source and fulfillment of all that our hearts long for. We find our way to Him.

SCRIPTURE

Deuteronomy 4:9; 6:4–7 | Psalm 36:8; 42:1; 145:4–5 | Isaiah 26:8

VII.

*"Though after my skin worms destroy this body,
yet in my flesh shall I see God."*

JOB 19:26 KJV

IT'S BEEN A FEW WEEKS since Mr. Dalton came with his tractor to turn the garden under. After we'd picked what we wanted, we took down the electric fence that rims the perimeter and left the rest for wildlife to forage. The garden was far from neat, full as it was of broken vines, rotting pumpkin, and dried corn stalk, but it contained its own kind of bounty. Then when everyone and everything had had their fill, our neighbor up the road came to till the remaining vegetation into the earth. And with that, the growing season was over.

But the work is not over, the work of late fall being the work of enriching the ground. It is the hidden work of decomposition and decay as microorganisms, insects, and bacteria break down organic matter and turn it into rich, life-giving soil. And in a reversal of everything we'd been doing to this point, instead of trying to keep plants alive, we'll now assist their decay. We'll use autumn's fallen leaves and a summer's worth of grass clippings to mulch; we'll continue to compost and find ways to return nitrogen and vital nutrients to the ground. But the real work will happen in darkness, where what once was alive returns to the earth that gave it life.

Thinking of all that's happening in the soil right now, I can't help but think of my own turning under, my own breaking down. The Scripture tells us that we came from the earth and we will return to the earth, and science tells us that our bodies are made from the very minerals under our feet. I think of the old cemetery that sits about three hundred yards from this garden. There's another in the center of our community and one by the church, but the one nearest us is a family cemetery, used by those who worked the ground that now holds them. I attended a burial there last summer. Eula still lived on family land near where my family lives now, and in the last days of her life, Nathan would wander down the lane to visit and pray with her. She'd been ill for a long time, her death certain.

Some days, I go up to the cemetery and walk among the dead. I do not find it a lonesome place. It speaks of grief and loss, but it is also peaceful, more garden than grave. The small plot is roughly an acre, shaded by a dozen trees, oaks, juniper, and cypress; and in spring, the graves are covered with periwinkle. But today, in late fall, they're blanketed in leaves, pine needles, and acorns slowly burrowing their way into the earth.

I walk through the graves carefully so as not to walk on the dead. To do so, my mother taught me, is disrespectful. In most places, it is easy enough to navigate the bodies under my feet, their loved ones having had the foresight to mark them with both head and foot stones. But in older sections, I find it impossible. There are too many unmarked, untended graves—too many stones decayed, washed away by wind and rain, to not find myself standing on the shoulders of the dead. Everything, it seems, is destined to return to soil, bit by bit, grain by grain, to return to the earth from which it came.

The stones I can read mark constellations of families and friends joined together in death as they were once in life: Blackburn, Spradlin, Weaver, Boulding, Blakenship, Gearhart, Niday. I read the dates and calculate who passed first and who sorrowed for them when they did. Who went on ahead and who was left behind? Which mothers lost sons, which husbands lost wives? Who wrote, "Weep not father and mother for me / For I am waiting in glory for thee"? And simply, "At rest"? Who had enough faith to understand that the dead had gotten the better end of the deal? Who chiseled these words in stone?

Peaceful in thy silent slumber
Peaceful in thy grave so low
Thou no more will join our number
Thou no more our sorrows know.

Who knew that in a grand reversal, the dead are to be envied? That they in their earthen beds, their bodies becoming one with the soil, are further along the journey to eternal life than we?

Because all soil, even the soil in a cemetery, promises life. And those who have become part of it lie like dormant seeds, planted and pressed and patted down. They lie waiting for the day when their bodies will rise and all those who dwell in dust wake up and shout with joy. They wait for the day "the earth will give birth to her dead."[40]

And if the cemetery is a kind of garden, the grave is also a kind of womb. Because if we, the living, were fashioned from earth, the dead are being refashioned within it. It is as mysterious as our own birth; but know this: the One who first made us in secret places of the earth will remake us in the same. Sown in corruption, we will be raised in incorruption. Sown a natural body, we will be raised a spiritual body. Because it is written, "Just as we have borne the image of the man of dust, we will also bear the image of the Man of Heaven."[41]

But for now, this garden lies quiet and still. For now, the work is hidden deep within the earth as organic matter transforms it into rich, life-giving soil. For now, the dead wait to be reborn, the people of dust wait to be made in the image of heaven.

As I turn to walk home and cross the dirt path, I see bone and flesh. Coming closer, I recognize the carcass of a white-tailed deer left above the ground but steadily returning to it. It's a six-point buck that did not make it across the road. Bits of fur and flesh cling to bone, but for the most part, it's been stripped by both fowl and fair. Its naked spine and ribs are exposed, and I can see a ball and socket that I should not be able to see. A row of grinning teeth and empty eyes stare up at me.

I do not want to die. I do not want my flesh and heart to decay, to become one with the earth from which I was taken. I can hardly imagine my own bones decomposing and crumbling to dust. And yet, like Eula's, my death is inevitable. One day I too will be laid into the ground, to be reformed and remade. I will join those who have already returned to earth, whose bones give life to the periwinkle and juniper. With them, my body will be sown in corruption, and with them, I will wait.

I will wait through winter's night. I will wait for spring and resurrection. I will wait until the Gardener comes to turn His soil over and bring us to life again.

SCRIPTURE

Genesis 3:19–20 | Job 19:25–27 | Psalm 73:25–26; 103:14–20; 139:13–16; 146:3
Isaiah 26:19 | 1 Corinthians 15:35–58

Winter

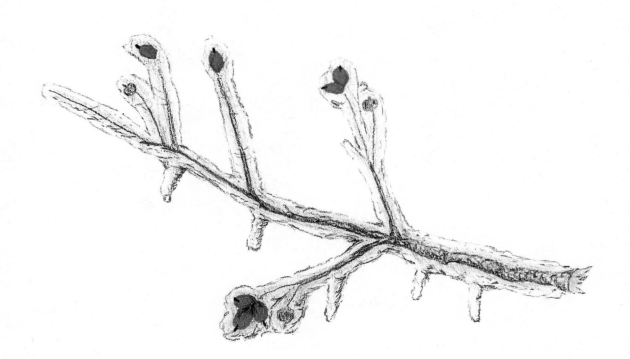

I.

*"The day is yours, and yours also the night; you established
the moon and the sun. It was you who set all the boundaries of the earth;
you made both summer and winter."*

PSALM 74:16—17

WINTER IS UPON US NOW. We're well past the killing frost, and the calendar tells me the season has changed, though mostly I know it's winter because of the darkness.

To be fair, it's a darkness that's been coming due since midsummer when the sun sat high and proud in the sky, and the light continued on and on and on. Forget equal time; give us the sun and only the sun and let us worship under it. We've been paying our tithes ever since, giving a minute here and a minute there; the loss so incremental we hardly noticed.

By autumn, we welcomed the earlier evenings as good for bonfires and quiet nights at home. And if we're honest, we were exhausted by summer's exuberance; the darkness settled us. But each day, more daylight slipped away. Each day, the night grew longer. We'd go to sleep in darkness and wake in the same. So that by the time the winter solstice came—that day when the earth's poles are tilted farthest from the sun—the difference between high summer and dark winter is the loss of over five hours of light.

No wonder you feel it in your bones. No wonder you know that winter has come.

I remember my dad talking of the gathering darkness with a sense of awe and sadness. "The shortest day of the year is coming," he'd say as if it were his duty to warn us. For him, the loss of daylight meant the loss of working hours and a certain despair settling over the earth. It wasn't the cold so much as the gloom that hung over the countryside, all gray and heaviness. We could only count on 160 days of sun per year (well below the national average of 205), and winter felt like a thief oppressing the poor. The landscape compounded things too. If you lived higher up in the mountains, you'd do well enough, but those who sat in the hollows and valleys wouldn't see the sun until it passed over the hills, sunup and sundown calculated by the geography that surrounded them.

Here in Virginia, we're more in line with the national average of sunny days, but winter's shadows still unnerve me. A kind of sheltering instinct kicks in; I withdraw and become less willing to venture out. I feel sleepier, and with the earth, I find myself shutting down. There are biological reasons, of course. The loss of light affects the body's natural circadian rhythm, that internal clock that's synchronized to the earth's revolutions and tells you when to wake and when to sleep. And although the changes are gradual, you can quickly find yourself in darkness not knowing how exactly you got there. In these moments, I find it hard to remember the light, and I begin to wonder if I imagined it all. I wonder if sun, warmth, and freedom were all in my head, a midsummer's dream.

Of course, there are ways to cope, as our friends further north can testify. The Danes have their *hygge* and the Dutch their *gezelligheid,* and the rest of us make do with climate control, interior lighting, and a stable food supply. We find solace in small comforts: a hot drink, candles, woolen socks, blankets, and books. But even our modern conveniences and hermetically sealed lives can't keep out the darkness. And before long, what we once welcomed as rest can become a kind of numbness; our seclusion, isolation; and the quietness, an echoing silence.

When the Creator first created, Genesis tells us that "darkness was over the surface of the deep,"[42] and all I can imagine is a cold, muddy, winter's night when nothing grows. But then, the Creator speaks, and light breaks through; and with the light comes sky and clouds, solid ground and seas, plants and animals, abundance and life. He separates the light and darkness and calls it morning and evening and puts sun, moon, and stars in the sky. But here's something I don't understand: God creates light, but He doesn't obliterate darkness. God brings light but lets the darkness stay.

Now I can tell you all the reasons why darkness is a good thing, how it allows for cycles of rest and dormancy, how it establishes day and night and helps us keep time. I can tell you how our bodies are set to its changes. I can tell you that certain things require darkness, that only certain things can be learned there. I can tell you that the stars shine brightest against a frozen winter sky, but this is all cold comfort when the nights are long and lonely.

So instead, I will tell you this: The Lord of Creation owns both the light and the darkness. He is Lord of both summer and winter, of good times and bad. To Him, day and night are alike. He has no circadian rhythm.

The One who rules over the darkness can't be overruled by yours.

Instead, He can enter into your night and be unshaken. He can make it "his covering, his canopy around him"[43] and be completely unharmed. So that while you wait for the days to lengthen, while you wait for the season to turn, while you wait for the dawn, the Lord of both light and dark can meet you there. Earth's longest night cannot hide you from His care. Earth's longest night cannot separate you from His love. Earth's longest night is light to Him.

Until one day when this same God—the One who sits in the gathering darkness with you—vanquishes darkness forever. Because as much as Genesis tells us of a God who made the light and tames the darkness, Revelation tells us of a God who extinguishes it altogether. And on that day, when earth and heaven finally align, night will be no more and winter's chill nothing but memory.

SCRIPTURE

Genesis 1:2–5 | 2 Samuel 22 | Psalm 74:16–23; 104:19–20
2 Chronicles 6:1 | Isaiah 45:2–3; 7–8 | Daniel 2:22 | Micah 7:8
Romans 8:35–39 | Revelation 21:22; 22:5

II.

*"He says to the snow, 'Fall on the earth' . . . So that everyone he has made
may know his work, he stops all people from their labor."*

JOB 37:6—7

———————————

THE SNOW FINALLY CAME DOWN last night. It's been forecast for over a week
now, ever since a mass of cold air began gathering itself in the north and became intent
on colliding with a system from the Gulf. For days, the skies have been low and heavy,
weighed down with moisture and expectation. But even if we knew it was coming, until
it did, no one could be sure of what it would mean. Obviously, the low lying areas would
have less accumulation than those at higher elevations, but besides that, all was conjecture.

We ended up with eleven inches through the night, enough to close the churches
on Sunday and the schools on Monday. I look out my bedroom window to a world
made new. With the storm passed, the sky is a rare blue, and sunlight glints off the
snow shrouding the muddy, frozen hills. The winter birds—junco, cardinal, and
titmouse—gather around the feeders. So light, they bounce across the snow in search
of seed and suet; their bony feet leave a trail of prints.

It's quiet, too. The fresh snow absorbs and dampens sound waves, creating an
eerie, if not serene, silence. Perhaps later, after it melts a bit and refreezes, this will

change, as sound echoes off its icy crust; but for now, all is calm. There are no vehicles on the road because it's still impassable, although I expect a truck from the Virginia Department of Transportation will plow through this afternoon, or maybe tomorrow. Either way, it doesn't matter. We've no place to go.

I make myself a cup of coffee and begin to plan what I will *not* do today. I will not wake the children until they wake themselves. I will not catch up on projects or chores. I will not do laundry. I will honor this day for what it is: a sabbath.

Sabbath is not a concept that the modern world has much appreciation for. Vacations we understand. Amusement and personal time, yes. But sabbath requires more from us than we're accustomed to giving, and a forced sabbath especially so. Forced sabbaths—those days when it seems like the elements and an elemental God conspire against us—mine us for more than we know how to give.

As forced sabbaths go, a snow day is gentle. They are temporary, and by this point in the year, I'm almost grateful for the pause. I even find voluntary, regular sabbaths, like those anticipated in Scripture, as something to look forward to because I can prepare and control them. Six days we labor, and when the seventh comes, we rest in the sure knowledge that we've worked and will work again.

But what about those forced sabbaths that linger? What about those days when we wait in unwanted dormancy? When we've lost a job and can't find another? When we're ill and nothing seems to help? What about those days, weeks, and months that drag on, when the only thing we want is to get back to business as usual but we can't?

To be laid low by forces outside our control, to be forced to inactivity against our wishes, is something else entirely.

And yet, even these days have purpose, exposing our deeper restlessness and testing how long we will keep faith, testing whether God is Himself faithful. Because this is the work that must, and can only, happen in dormancy. When our ability to work is stripped away, when we find ourselves in the dead of winter, we can finally discover what we've been trusting in. As our hope for the future falters, we learn whether we have placed or misplaced it. And as we cede control over our days, months, and years, we discern the limits of our power and the extent of His.

Later today, I'll take a quart of soup off the shelf. Perhaps two. The jar holds the season's abundance—potatoes, corn, beans, tomatoes—along with bits of venison from the hunt, carefully prepared and preserved months ago when the sun was high and the days long. I'll pop the lid and pour it into the Dutch oven and let it simmer. Today, we'll be warmed and fed and do no work.

Tomorrow we may hike in the woods because they are different in the snow, when the trees are stark and the ground covered in white. We'll lace our boots and layer our clothes and find warm gloves and stocking hats. If we go early enough, we'll be the first to cut the trail and leave our prints along the path; we'll feel like adventurers in a world

yet explored. Our breath will come hot and heavy, our cheeks redden with cold. We'll see the air as it escapes our lungs and condenses in front of us. The tip of my nose will freeze, and I'll remember it again.

But that is tomorrow. Today, we will rest. Today, we will wait. Today, we will sabbath, trusting His work and not our own.

SCRIPTURE

Deuteronomy 5:12–15 | Job 37:6–10 | Proverbs 25:13; 31:21
Hebrews 4:9–10

III.

"You crowned them with glory and honor and put everything under their feet . . . Yet at present we do not see everything subject to them. But we do see Jesus."

HEBREWS 2:7—9

A FEW WEEKS AGO, we cut a seven-foot Fraser fir, dragged it into our living room, and decorated it with bits of fabric and metal. I decked the mantle with evergreen and fruit—oranges, apples, pears, and cranberries on a string—and thought it the most natural thing in the world. Then I discovered a mouse in my kitchen and remembered that I am a hypocrite.

It's a curious thing, this bringing the outside world in. We're only comfortable with it within certain bounds—as long as the flowers are in vases, the animals tamed, and the breezes purified and temperate. But when nature comes in uninvited, when she runs along the baseboard, behind the refrigerator, and across a few feet of linoleum to burrow under the stove, we're less than hospitable. Still, it took me days to decide whether to set a trap. *Wasn't she only doing what came naturally to her? Wasn't she, like me, just trying to survive this cruel, cold world? Who can blame her for finding the warmth of a holiday kitchen inviting? What else was she supposed to do when crumbs of bread, pie, and cake catch in the corners?*

In the end, I never did decide to set a trap because Nathan asks no such questions and did it for me.

Of course, I know the answers as they've been presented to me. We are to rule over the earth. We are to rule over the fish of the sea, the birds of the air, and the mice of our kitchens. God has crowned us with glory and honor and given us dominion. But what does dominion look like east of Eden? What are we to do when the entire world seems to be at odds with itself, when creation is under a curse and we are too? What does dominion actually mean when all I've ever seen is conflict and struggle?

Within a few days, the tree began to decay as all things cut off from the earth do. Needles dropped to the floor, and the branches sagged under the weight of our celebration. Eventually, we took it out the same door we'd brought it in, but not before plucking a few immature cones and an unusual growth from its branches.

These we put downstairs in our nature collection, a curio dedicated to the curious: seashells, feathers, shelf fungus, seed pods, crystals, fossils in sandstone, and abandoned nests and turtle shells. I like nature. I truly do. But I especially like it inert and cataloged.

And yet, the world grows wild around us, like a vine wrapping itself up, under, over, and through a stone wall until it slowly breaks it apart. The mice find their way into my kitchen.

The spiders spin their webs in the corners of my bedroom. And then this happened: six weeks after we'd taken the tree outside, in the middle of winter when the world was frozen in ice, the branch in our basement erupted, giving birth to hundreds of tiny green praying mantises.

And once again, nature had won. Once again, nature exercised *her* dominion and asked the simple question, "Who's in charge here, really?"

For all our answers, maybe the real question that we and the mice and the trees are trying to answer is this: Who's in charge here anyway? Who gets to have their say? Who gets to rule over this earth? Maybe, that's where the war and fighting comes from, just as James says it does.

In the book of Revelation, we're given a vision of a new earth, of the holy city, New Jerusalem coming down like a bride. They tell me that this means the city replaces the Garden, that Eden is finally domesticated and comes under the rule of humankind as it was always meant to. I think I believe this, but I've also never seen a city where death doesn't reign. No city I know has a river, unpolluted, clear as crystal. No city I know has streets lined with trees that heal the nations. I've never seen humankind rule anything but with oppression and force.

And so I wonder, does the city replace the Garden? Or do we finally become the kind of people who can live peaceably in a garden? Does nature finally surrender to us? Or does the curse lift because we've both come under the rule of One greater than either of us?

Colossians 1 tells us about the Ruler of this new place, the One who can make both heaven and earth, and man and beast bow before Him:

> For in him all things were created:
> things in heaven and on earth,
> visible and invisible,
> whether thrones or powers or rulers or authorities;
> all things have been created through him and for him. . . .
> through him to reconcile to himself all things,
> whether things on earth or things in heaven,
> by making peace through his blood, shed on the cross.[44]

As much as we believe we're taming nature—maybe that we are even called to tame it—we must not forget that we ourselves are being tamed. We are being brought under the rule of nature's Christ; and only when we are, can we rule well. Only when we submit to our Lord can our rule become the stewardship it's meant to be.

So we will wait for this day together, the mice and trees and the praying mantis and me. We will wait for the day when God's sons will be revealed and everything is finally and fully subject to Him. We will wait for the day when the entire world—man and beast and tree—can finally rest in heavenly peace.

SCRIPTURE

Genesis 1:28–30 | Psalm 8 | Isaiah 65:17–19 | Romans 8:19–25
Colossians 1:15–20 | Hebrews 2:5–9 | Revelation 21:1–4; 22

IV.

"My Father is the gardener. He cuts off every branch in me that bears no fruit, while every branch that does bear fruit he prunes so that it will be even more fruitful."

JOHN 15:1—2

I PULLED UP THE DRIVE YESTERDAY only to find Nathan hacking away at the peach trees, piles of branches accumulating around his feet. It was a bit of a mismatch, a grown man wielding forged steel against the trees' bare limbs. Tender shoots that only a few months earlier had born fruit now lay on the ground, cut off, dashed to the earth. And then I realized that he's done the same with the grapevine, the apple trees, and the fig.

The brutality of pruning always shocks me even if the concept is simple enough. In the first seasons of a plant's life, cutting back new growth redirects vital energy to the roots. Instead of producing a lot of leaves, blossoms, and fruit, the plant produces the strong, stable root system necessary for future growth. Once the plant is established, pruning over subsequent seasons allows the gardener to remove dead and diseased portions. It also allows you to shape the plant or tree in a way that is both beautiful and productive. But like other traumatic tending (such as transplanting), you should prune when plants are dormant, usually sometime in late winter.

This much I understand. Limit a plant's production in its earliest years for the sake of future production. Remove dead and diseased branches to preserve the whole. Shape it into a thing of beauty.

The part of pruning that I can't grasp, the part that's entirely counterintuitive, is cutting back good branches on well-established trees. Especially in winter. Especially when you have so little hope to begin with. *Why, when the tree is at its most vulnerable, its limbs bare and exposed, would you come along with sharpened shears? Shouldn't you preserve the shoots and branches? Shouldn't you protect and celebrate the season's growth?*

I watch as Nathan continues to cut away, and I'm tempted to intervene, to ask him if he thinks that maybe, possibly, he's cut enough and that he doesn't need to cut more. But I don't, and another branch falls to the earth. Stepping back, he assesses his work. The tree is almost half the size it was an hour ago. It hardly looks like a tree with its limbs amputated as they are. But if he's done his job right, he will have cut back at least 50 percent of this year's new growth. All that work, all that effort, all those hopes, all those dreams—gone.

Satisfied, Nathan cleans his shears and moves to the next tree.

I suppose pruning requires more courage and faith than I have—courage to cut what needs to be cut and faith to believe that the cut will bring life and growth. Were I to prune these peach trees, I'd cut them the same way I cut Nathan's hair when we were newlyweds: with a timidity that was simultaneously never enough and too much. But Nathan knows what he's doing, he knows just when and how and where to cut. And like any good gardener, he cares more about the flourishing of the tree than sentimentality. He knows that failure to prune is failure to care. And he's not lured by the promise of quick and easy fruit.

In John 15, Jesus tells His disciples that the Father is also a faithful Gardener who cares for His own. He cares so much that He cuts them. He cuts away the bad and burns it; He also cuts the good to stimulate growth. But it's the kind of growth that takes time, the kind that goes against your natural instinct to preserve growth at any cost. Instead, the Father is concerned with fruit that lasts. He's concerned with good fruit.

This doesn't make much sense to people who honor quantity over quality, who want it to come fast and quick. Always onward and upward. Always expanding. More productivity. More gains. More profit. Instead, pruning prefers healthy growth and knows that flourishing is not a race. Pruning knows that abundance in the future often requires loss in the present.

By now, I'm not thinking of peach trees or grape vines or figs. I'm thinking of lost dreams, lost hopes, and lost desires. I'm thinking of all those things that have been taken from me. All those things that were cut away.

I had dreams of fruitfulness, dreams like tender shoots, growing from the very center of my being. They were not dreams of vanity, pride, or lust. They were hopes for goodness and flourishing. And then they were cut off. Out of nowhere, with no explanation, cold steel cut through my flesh, slicing, marring, disfiguring. I stood limbs outstretched, exposed, and embarrassed. I had been audacious enough to hope, audacious enough to send out a shoot, and now it lays on the ground, dead.

Was it for disease that I was cut or was it for growth, and how would I know the difference? And does it even matter when the loss feels the same?

I'm thinking too of how often pruning happens right when you feel like you can't take any more, when you're already in a season of dormancy and the world around you lies gray and lifeless. But it's in these late winter days that the Gardener can see most clearly, when the cover of your fig leaves are gone and you stand naked before Him. And when He's done His work, don't be surprised that you're half the person you knew yourself to be.

Jesus tells us that our Father Gardener prunes us for our fruitfulness, and the writer of Hebrews tells us this same Father chastens those He loves. And I believe this, but it still hurts, and most days, I don't have the courage or the faith to believe that this is for my best. Too many days, I want the old part of me back because it is familiar. I forget that losing my life is the only way to find it; I forget that I've been cut to be made whole.

But some days, I remember. Some days I remember the taste of sweet, ripe peaches and clusters of purple grapes. I remember that Nathan did this last year. I remember that we've been through this before. I've seen these trees and vines cut back, and I've seen these same trees and vines grow back. I've seen them stripped down, and I've seen them flourish again. I remember that I've got peaches in my freezer and jam on my shelf and hope for more. I remember that abundance and life came from the cut.

SCRIPTURE

Leviticus 19:23–25; 25:3–4 | Job 1:21 | Isaiah 2:4; 5:6; 18:4–6
Micah 4:3 | Matthew 16:24–25 | John 15:2–8 | Hebrews 12:5–6
James 1:2–4

V.

"Look at the birds of the air; they do not sow or reap or store away in barns, and yet your heavenly Father feeds them. Are you not much more valuable than they?"

MATTHEW 6:26

OUR CAT SAUNTERED INTO breakfast this morning, covered in feathers. It seems he'd already had his.

By now, it's late winter, and the birds are starting to return, drawn by the lengthening days and the feeders that sit in our backyard. At the right moment, I can look out my kitchen window and see a veritable aviary. Goldfinches cluster around sacks of nyjer while downy and red-bellied woodpeckers feast on suet. Closer to the house, blue jays, catbirds, sparrows, titmice, cardinals, chickadees, and juncos gorge on sunflower and corn.

But our cat also sits in the backyard, long and sleek, hidden behind planters and among the bushes. He crouches low, predatory and patient.

A few years ago, I bought a blue collar with a small bell and put it on his neck. It seemed the least I could do. After all, we were the ones who'd set up feeders.

We were the ones who'd filled them with milo and millet, sunflower and corn, and I didn't like to think of myself as the kind of hostess who'd invite her guests to slaughter. At first the bell worked, but then the laws of physics came into play: the collar broke ("nature tends toward disorder"), and I did not buy another one ("an object at rest will stay at rest until acted upon by an outside force").

Nathan says I shouldn't worry about how we've disrupted the ecosystem. He says that the birds we're feeding are more numerous than the birds we're feeding to the cat. I know he's right, at least on the level of accounting. All things considered, we're in the black. *So why am I so bothered when I find the cat covered in death and a house finch covered in blood, its eye darkened?*

This is normal, I tell myself. This is the state of things. Creation groans under the curse, awaiting redemption. Why should I worry about what a cat will do? I remember that I hunt and stalk and kill too. But then I remember that I am also hunted, and maybe this is the real source of my anxiety.

Maybe I'm not so concerned with what kills as with what is killed.

I know that I'm no less vulnerable than the birds that feed outside my window. In them, I see my own fragility, all bones and feathers and lighter than air. Yes, there is intelligence, beauty, and grace; but there's also a kind of anxiety that flits and flutters and flies at the slightest shadow. Because one minute you'll be feeding on abundance, and the next, the cat will pounce.

Perhaps this is why Jesus calls us to give attention to the birds, both to how they live and how they die. In the gospel of Matthew, He says:

> "Do not worry about your life, what you will eat or drink; or about your
> body, what you will wear. . . . Look at the birds of the air; they do not sow
> or reap or store away in barns, and yet your heavenly Father feeds them.
> Are you not much more valuable than they?"[45]

By heaven's accounting, the fact that birds eat the finest seed is not testament to my care for them, but to the Father's. And the fact that He provides for them means that He will provide for me too. Just as He uses me to lay a feast in the presence of their enemies, He'll use a multitude of means to lay one for me in the presence of mine. And if the birds of the air don't worry, why should I? Aren't I worth more than they?

But then I think, it's one thing to trust the Father with your life; it's another to trust Him with your death. It's one thing to trust that He'll set up feeders on which you can feast; it's another thing to remember that your enemy waits, crouching low and silent beneath them. But again, Jesus calls us to give attention to the birds:

> "Do not be afraid of those who kill the body but cannot kill the soul. . . .
> Are not two sparrows sold for a penny? Yet not one of them
> will fall to the ground outside your Father's care. . . .
> So don't be afraid; you are worth more
> than many sparrows."[46]

I read in Isaiah of a coming peaceable kingdom, when the lion eats straw and lies down with the lamb, when the child plays on the serpent's nest. When the cat does not need a bell. I read of a coming peaceable kingdom when "they will not harm or destroy each other"[47] and such primal fear is no more. But this kingdom has not yet come.

And so as we pray for it, we must also learn to live in its absence. We must learn what the birds teach us: Do not be afraid. Trust your Father with your life, and trust Him with your death. The One who provides all you need for this life will provide all you need for the next. Are you not worth more than many sparrows?

SCRIPTURE

Isaiah 11:6–9 | Isaiah 65:24–25 | Matthew 6:25–26
Matthew 10:28–31 | 1 Peter 5:8

VI.

*"A shoot will come up from the stump of Jesse; from his roots a Branch will bear fruit . . . .
The nations will rally to him, and his resting place will be glorious."*

ISAIAH 11:1, 10

SIX WEEKS AFTER I WATCHED Nathan prune the peach trees, I watched a different man take down a sycamore. It was a hundred winters old and ten feet around. I'd seen woodpeckers and hawks in its branches. In summer, it bloomed green, reaching across the sky and stretching beneath the earth. Come fall, its yellow leaves shined like gold against the clear blue sky. But it was marked to come down this winter Saturday. I don't know why, and I suppose there was a reason. (There always is.) It stood just yards from our property line, but because it wasn't my tree, no one asked me.

The man working to fell it was young and lean. He wore a grimy white t-shirt, pants too large and loose to be safe, and after the second rope snapped, a cigarette from his lip. He brandished a chainsaw but had no protective gear, no guards or helmet, nothing to shield him except his own confidence.

He was removing the low hanging branches when I first noticed him, the whine of his saw drawing my attention. *Were these limbs diseased, threatening the health of the tree?* I wondered. *Or was there some secret rot that I could not see?* Some trees must come down, especially those so weak that any passing storm would topple them.

It's best to drop such trees in controlled conditions, when you can direct where they will land. To do this, you clear the limbs below shoulder height. Then you cut a notch in the direction you want the tree to fall. It should have an upper cut that penetrates a quarter of the tree's diameter and a lower cut that meets to form a wedge. On the other side of the tree, directly opposite this notch, you make a felling cut. Done right, geometry and physics take care of the rest.

But nothing about this was being done right. The young man continued to hack away at the branches, bits of forged steel tearing through their supple flesh. Then, without warning, he lifted the chainsaw high and plunged it straight into a broad limb that extended over his head. Pierced, water and life flowed from the cut. *What was I seeing? Water gushing from a tree?* But then I remembered: the sap was running.

Toward the end of winter, as spring comes on, daytime temperatures rise above freezing while nighttime temperatures stay below. This daily fluctuation initiates a cycle of freezing and thawing within trees that sets off a parallel fluctuation in the pressure systems at a molecular level. These changes draw water from the roots up through the trunks to the branches. During this time of sap rising (usually 4–6 weeks), you can "tap" into a tree, and sap will run out the wound, drop by drop. Collect enough of it, and you can boil it down to sweet syrup.

But the sap did not drip from the sycamore when the young man cut into it; it gushed. And when I saw him do this, I knew the tree was full of life. I also knew it would fall.

In Scripture, cutting a tree down is often a sign of judgment. Not always, of course; trees are also harvested for construction, craft, and heat. But the image of "laying the ax to the root," as John the Baptist puts it, is particularly reserved for those trees that do not bring forth good fruit. "Look," Isaiah writes, speaking of nations that God will judge, "the Lord GOD of Armies will chop off the branches with terrifying power, and the tall trees will be cut down, the high trees felled."[48]

In other words, if you can know a tree by its fruit, you can also know whether you should cut a tree down by whether its fruit is good or bad. To cut down a tree is to render judgment on it, to determine it a fruitless, faithless tree. So established is this principle that the opposite is also true. When the Israelites besieged a city, for example, the law forbade them from cutting down fruitful trees. Instead of destroying them, they were to steward them.

By late afternoon, the hundred year old sycamore had been notched and ropes tied from its trunk and branches to the back of an old pickup. The young, lean man approached the tree from behind to make his felling cut. He began, but the blade, tired from hours of work, quickly sputtered and died. He cursed and pulled the starter, one, two, three, four times before it came to life again. He deepened the cut a few inches more, and then stepped away, calling for the truck to move.

On the signal, the engine roared and jumped forward. The ropes pulled taut, but the tree stood unwavering. Then without warning, the yellow rope broke. The man cursed that the tree should have come down and called for the truck to stop. He collected the bits of frayed rope and tied them to themselves. Then gingerly, he moved toward the tree with his saw. Poking the noisy blade into the felling cut, he widened it, pressing deep into the flesh. Even from a distance, I could see the pulverized bits of sycamore flying around his bare arms and exposed face. Stepping away again, he called for the truck to move. "Slower this time!" he barked. The truck inched forward, the ropes strained, but the tree remained, tall and upright.

Then the second rope—the black one—snapped, and there was no saving it, tied as it was to a branch higher on the tree. Again, he swore and cursed the tree. Across the way, a neighbor stepped out onto her porch and then stepped back in. The man who'd commissioned the work came to see. None of the other trees had resisted this way, but then none of the others had lived this way.

Taking his saw again, the young man circled the tree, his movements anxious and uncertain, thrusting here and now, there. He decided to enlarge the notch again, a gamble to be sure, should the tree choose that moment to fall. I watched, praying that it wouldn't.

Finally, he put down his saw and picked up his ax. Gathering his strength, he swung against the felling cut; the impact of the blade echoed through the hills. Again and again, deeper and deeper. And then he stopped. Sweat pouring down his face, he lifted a weary arm and flicked his wrist. The rope strained. The tree quivered. And from deep within its heart came a groan and seismic crack. Wood splintered as grain tore from grain. It was finished.

A week later I learned why the tree came down. The owner didn't want it anymore. There was no disease, no threat. He just didn't want it anymore.

Today, months later, the hundred-year-old sycamore lies in pieces around its stump, its limbs and trunk butchered. The weeds have grown up among the debris, and a mockingbird nests in the piles of brush. But she's too low to the ground, and my cat stalks her young. There's a grief here. A senseless destruction. Good trees should not be cut down.

But isn't this exactly the plight of the world we inhabit? Isn't this exactly the struggle? That good is deemed evil and evil good? That those who should live are cut down and those who should be felled aren't? And isn't this exactly what the Anointed One suffered, He who did no wrong and yet was counted among the evil doers? Isn't this exactly what He endured when He was cut off from the land of the living by oppression and judgment?

Isn't this exactly why He hung on a tree?

I went out to the stump today and counted the rings. It's still a hundred years old. It still lies scarred and brutalized. But then I noticed something. Tiny green shoots are coming up around the base and more are coming from the side. The tree is not dead. Deep beneath the earth, the roots hold life within them still.

And isn't this exactly the hope of the world? Isn't this exactly the longing? That good will conquer evil and evil fall? That we who should live will rise and devils who should be felled will be? And isn't this exactly what the Anointed One promises, He who did no wrong and yet was counted among the evil doers? Isn't this exactly what He restored when He was brought again to the land of the living by resurrection and justice?

Isn't this exactly why He rose from the grave?

SCRIPTURE

Genesis 2:9 | Deuteronomy 20:19–20 | Isaiah 10:33–34; 11:1–10; 53:2, 8–9
Ezekiel 17:22–24; 31 | Matthew 3:10; 7:16–20

VII.

"Very truly I tell you, unless a kernel of wheat falls to the ground and dies, it remains only a single seed. But if it dies, it produces many seeds."

JOHN 12:24

HE SITS IN THE CORNER, in a chair beside the fireplace. He's holding a pencil and legal pad, piles of seed packets, and gardening catalogs at his feet. Today's been a gray day, and we've been stuck inside. A winter rain pelts against the windows reminding us that the season has not yet released its grip. But we're content to stay in our place, waiting out the cold, taking comfort in our catalogs and plans.

Nathan asks me what I want to plant this year. We talk about what did well last and what we eat and how each crop stores. We discuss whether we want to give precious space to corn or just buy it from the co-op. We'll plant tomatoes, cucumbers, peppers, and squash. We'll put in cold crops first, of course, and we always plant peas.

Thinking of peas, I remember the farmer's son turned cleric-scientist, Friar Mendel, out in his garden with his peas, selecting and propagating them over their generations. Mendel's work became the basis of modern genetics, and in some way, has led to my sitting in my living room on a cold winter afternoon sorting through seed catalogs. Because of cross pollination and breeding, I can choose between seeds that grow small tomatoes, yellow tomatoes, purple tomatoes, sauce tomatoes, tomatoes that bloom early, tomatoes that bloom late, or tomatoes that grow to the size of a dinner plate.

Chemical companies got into the game too, creating seeds that can withstand their own particular herbicides, thus leading to higher yield. But they've also patented the technology so when their seed falls into the ground and produces an abundant crop, you dare not save any of that seed to plant next year or you'll find yourself under a lawsuit. The seed you hold in your hand is proprietary property, and you've only bought one life cycle. You'll have to come back again if you want another. But it makes me wonder, *Is the patent because the seed lives or because it doesn't die? Are they trading in life or in death?*

Modern agriculture may have given us the ability to select our seeds and feed more with less, but it can't escape the fundamental questions of life on this earth. It can't change the question of nature warring against itself and with us. What varieties will survive and how? Who's to say which traits are desirable? And who's in charge of all of this anyway? Who owns the fecundity of a seed?

Because here's the thing about a seed, here's the math of exponential growth: an average kernel of corn will produce one stalk, which when fertilized, can produce one to two ears, each of which hold an average of eight hundred kernels. With a ratio of 1:1600, no wonder propagation is big business. No wonder you must protect your seed.

In considering nature's fertility, author Annie Dillard questions whether it's proof that the world is bent toward competition and destruction; she writes that "evolution loves death more than it loves you or me."[49] There's something to this. Nature doesn't care about the individual seed or plant. It only cares about the survival of the species and will happily sacrifice you if it needs to. The fecundity of a seed, then, is the calculus of death. The cicadas emerge en masse because they know many will be eaten, and with enough, some will survive. So it is with pollen, eggs, and seed; nature knows that only a few will fertilize and actually produce life. So it creates millions of them.

After all, I'm not the only one preparing for the coming spring. I'm not the only one planning my seed. Right now, the winter soil holds billions of seeds waiting to sprout. Right now, acorns and maple keys lie in the ground. Dandelion and goldenrod rest in darkness. Violet and wild oat bide their time. Right now, the earth is a storehouse of life.

What are we to make of this? That only the fittest survive and only the fittest deserve to live? Or does the world, like us, groan and struggle and limp her way to *life*?

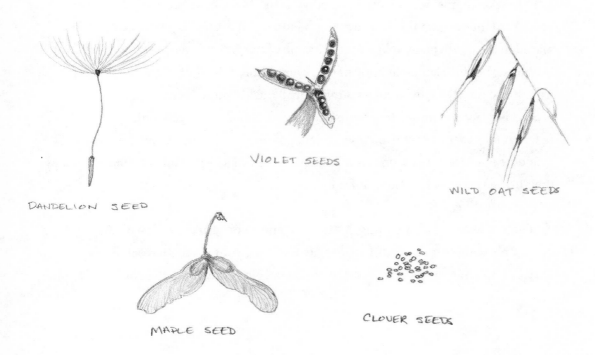

VIOLET SEEDS

DANDELION SEED

WILD OAT SEEDS

MAPLE SEED

CLOVER SEEDS

I do not believe the universe rests on the survival of the fittest. I do not believe we earn our right to life. Think this way, and your days here will be nothing more than an exercise in existential self-justification, a works salvation. Make death ultimate, and you'll have to spend your days arguing why you deserve to live. But you do not live because you deserve to; you do not live because your ancestors' seed made it through a biological gauntlet. You live because your Creator gave you life. You live because He is a God of life, and while nature might struggle to care about you, He does not.

The only way to be at peace in this world, then, is to become people inclined toward life. The only way to be at peace with a God of life is to plan for life and expect it to break through. Against all odds, we must bet on life. Keep your Monte Carlo and Vegas. Give me a piece of ground and a forest and a year's time, and I'll risk it all.

But make no mistake; life on this earth is a risk. Make no mistake; death will be your constant companion, and one day you too will die. One day, your body will be placed in the earth, planted like a seed. I think of the graves three hundred yards from my house, bodies planted in hope of the resurrection. I think of all the life that came from those now lying in darkness. I think of all the life yet to come.

And now we can understand Jesus' words: "Very truly I tell you, unless a kernel of wheat falls to the ground and dies, it remains only a single seed. But if it dies, it produces many seeds. Anyone who loves their life will lose it, while anyone who hates their life in this world will keep it for eternal life."[50]

Life. Life. Life.

If nature teaches you anything, it's that you must concern yourself with life, and not simply your own. You must so love life that even your death serves it. Because what nature knows is that one life does not stand alone any more than one seed stands alone. Your life stands in the generations. And one day, the generations planted in hope will rise together. One day, we will live as our Redeemer does. One day, together, we shall see Him standing upon the dust; we will, in our flesh, see our God.

Today is not that day, however. Today, it is still winter. Today, the wind and rain blow cold. So what are you to do? What are you to do while you wait?

This is what you do in winter: you plan for spring.

This is what you do when the earth lies dark: you plan for dawn.

This is what you do when death seems to reign: you plan for resurrection.

SCRIPTURE

Genesis 1:11, 28–29 | Job 19:25–27 | Ecclesiastes 11:6
Matthew 16:25 | Mark 8:35 | John 12:23–26 | Romans 8:18–25
1 Corinthians 15:35–38 | Galatians 6:7–9

Learning to Listen:
A Field Guide

IN PSALM 19, David writes, "The heavens declare the glory of God; the skies proclaim the work of his hands. Day after day they pour forth speech; night after night they reveal knowledge. They have no speech, they use no words; no sound is heard from them. Yet their voice goes out into all the earth, their words to the ends of the world."[51]

In this book, I've tried to communicate something of what I've heard the heavens say. But more than simply retelling our conversation, I want to invite you to listen yourself. I want you to learn to hear the message that has gone out to the whole earth, the message that is meant for you as much as for me.

But hearing the testimony of nature can be difficult, especially for those who live in the modern world. For us, nature is more white noise or applause track than dialogue partner. And even those who can hear its voice can't always make out what's been said, the message lost in translation. If the psalmist is correct, however, if nature is trying to tell us something about the Creator, we must learn to listen to it. If our hearts are to be turned, our ears must first be tuned.

With that goal, here are ten principles that guide my own process of listening to nature's witness. I trust they will help you along yours.

1. Begin by understanding that the natural world is good. There is a deep, inherent beauty, and right-ness built into its order, cycles, rhythms, and purposes. The Creator has designed the universe to work in certain ways, through seasons of rest and flourishing, cycles of life, death, and resurrection. And, as such, you shouldn't be surprised when you see truth embodied in creation. Know too that the natural world is sustained by a common grace that brings the rain on both the just and unjust. Because of this, both those who already know Him and those who are simply seeking, can find Him here. Day by day, He is revealing something of Himself to all who will listen.

2. As you observe creation, remember that you are also looking at a world groaning for redemption. While the natural world is good, it is also trapped in what the apostle Paul deems "futility" or "frustration."[52] This means that you must neither minimize nature's brokenness, nor baptize it. Given amenities like climate control, food delivery, and modern medicine, it's possible to inoculate ourselves from some of the harshest realities of life and adopt a sentimental attitude toward nature. But if we expect to find Eden, we'll be shocked when we find life in the wild "nasty, brutish, and short."[53]

At the same time, nature's harshness is not her factory setting, nor her coming end. Creatures may be driven by base needs of hunger, thirst, and reproduction. They may fight for domination and territorial control; scarcity may reign. But is this the created order or the cursed order? Or both? Scripture teaches that the natural world exists in a space between the goodness that was and the goodness that will be, and just because something happens in nature doesn't mean it should. Hearing nature's voice means hearing it as both praise and lament.

3. Remember that you are part of the natural world, that your body and its placement in creation is part of God's design. While human beings have a kind of stewardship of the earth, and in some sense stand apart from it, we are also creatures. We too have been made. We too reveal the patterns of His goodness. As you observe the world around you, pay attention to how you inhabit nature and how nature interacts and adapts to you. Pay attention to both the responsibilities and limits of your stewardship. Consider what it means to live within an ecosystem that can be both blessed and harmed by your presence.

4. Intentionally engage with the natural world. Open your window. Put down your phone. Go outside. This may sound simple, but in our modern context, it's entirely possible to awaken inside your home, walk through your garage to a vehicle, and proceed to an office or school having never exposed yourself to the elements. Because of this, you must intentionally interact with nature. You do not have to move to the country or even walk to the park (although I recommend both), but you must give attention to the grass growing between the cracks in the sidewalk. The sky and clouds above your head. The day's temperature and precipitation. The flower on your windowsill. The bird you hear but cannot see. Your own body. All of these are sources of natural revelation. Learning from them is less about location and more about perception.

5. As you are able, spend extended time in nature. While nature is always speaking, it is also important to have time for dedicated conversation. Take a hike, go camping, or spend an evening lying under the stars instead of sitting in front of the television. Or simply find a spot—your spot—and stay there for as long as you can. Sit on a bench, a log, a rock, and quiet yourself. If you can't get outside, take a potted plant and simply observe it. Watch and note what you see. Use your five senses to observe colors, textures, smells, and patterns. The first few minutes will most likely be small talk, but as you settle in, you'll begin to hear unexpected things.

6. Pay attention to details. Sketch or write out a description of a seed, a tree, or an insect. These exercises force you to slow down and observe what you'd naturally rush past. Give yourself permission to delight in the spots of a ladybug or the whiskers on your cat. Lose yourself in the underside of a leaf, tracing its veins and patterns. All while asking yourself, "What does this say about the Creator? What glory does this reveal?"

7. **Don't miss the big picture.** As you pay attention to details, place them in context of their ecosystem. Look at the tree from which the leaf fell. Observe how it branches from roots to trunk to boughs. See what nests in it, what grows underneath and on it. Watch as different parts of the environment relate to each other. Consider how a change in one would affect the other. By doing this, you'll gain appreciation for the interconnectedness of all things as well as the ingenuity and power of the God who holds them together.

8. **Return to the same place throughout the day and year so you can observe nature through different times, seasons, and cycles of life.** Plant a garden or stake out a particular patch of ground, a bush, or perhaps a tree. Observe it in the morning and evening and before and after a storm. Watch as the light shifts and the shadows with them. Notice how nothing stays the same, how change is the only constant. Record your observations over time and track the differences. Or if you keep a personal journal, consider noting the day's weather in it or what you saw in nature that day as a way to connect the seasonal changes around you with the changes in your own life.

9. **Think about what you see and be curious.** Ask yourself questions that you do not yet—or may never—know the answer to. *Why is this leaf green but that one is red? Why is the bird's wing shaped this way? How does that fungus stay attached to the tree?* Make a list of things you wonder about, and later, read and research them, discovering what others have already learned. Then try to assimilate your new knowledge of nature with what you know about other fields of study. Think about how the natural world parallels the truths found in theology, art, music, and engineering.

And finally, for the hardest part . . .

10. Allow yourself to feel small. Let yourself be awed and humbled by all you don't know and all you can't control. Being stewards of the earth does not mean that we have power over it or even that we understand it. Instead, stewardship means serving the One who does. Because more often than not, giving attention to the creation will remind you of the Creator, and with David in Psalm 8, you'll be left asking, "When I consider your heavens, the work of your fingers . . . what is mankind that you are mindful of them, human beings that you care for them?"[54]

In the end, nature exists for the same reason that you and I do—to praise and rejoice in the God who made us. So when the trees clap their hands in full color and the heavens declare goodness through day and night, they teach us to raise our voices too. They teach us to sing with our words and bodies and lives: "Lord, our Lord, how majestic is your name in all the earth!"[55]

And when we do, it's the most natural thing in all the world.

Acknowledgments

IN GOD'S GRACE, none of us journey through life alone. We are grateful to those who have made this book and our time on earth full of life, love, and beauty. May our turning days bring us closer to Him and each other.

Phoebe, Harry, and Peter, you understand that life with dad and mom means countless nature walks, art museums, and used bookstores (especially on vacation). We love you desperately.

Friends and family, you've bought our books and cheered us on from afar.

The Ds, especially Melinda who might love the land even more than we do.

Daniel, for your kindness to the Anderson kids (and the Anderson parents). Your friendship is magic.

Michelle Berg Radford, your support, advice, and camaraderie are a beautiful, unexpected gift.

Erin, we started talking together five years ago and still have so many things to say.

Heather, Wendy, Bekah, and Rachael, friends on the journey.

Erik W., partner in this work of writing.

The team at Moody Publishers—Judy, Amanda, Ashley, Kathryn, and especially Erik P., who caught the artistic vision for this book from the beginning and patiently answered every question we had. It would not be the book it is without your work and collaboration.

The Art Department of Floyd County High School, for first inspiring a gangly teenage boy with the joy of art.

The Roanoke Valley Bird Club, for the birds.

And finally, readers of *Humble Roots* who first convinced us that there was so much more to say about this wild, beautiful world God has made.

Notes

---

1. William Blake, "Auguries of Innocence," in *The Complete Poetry and Prose of William Blake*, David V. Erdman and Harold Bloom, eds. (Berkeley: University of California Press, 2008), 490.

2. Carl Sandberg, "Fog," in *Selected Poems*, George and Willene Hendrick, eds. (San Diego: Harcourt Brace, 1996), 37.

3. Luke 13:6–9.

4. George Gordon, Lord Byron, "The Destruction of Sennacherib," in *Lord Byron: Selected Poems*, Peter J. Manning and Susan J. Wolfson, eds. (London: Penguin Books, 2005), 355.

5. The American poet Emily Dickinson often used nature to represent themes of life, death, and suffering. While she employs the image of the robin in other poems in a more carefree manner, she penned a poem in 1862 with the opening line, "I dreaded that first Robin, so" that explores the disconnect between her internal life of grief and suffering with spring's promise of hope and resurrection.

6. Hebrews 11:1.

7. Genesis 8:22.

8. Job 38:36 (CSB).

9. Genesis 2:6 (NKJV).

10. Exodus 16:31.

11. Proverbs 30:8–9.

12. Obituary of Kenneth Marden Sewell, *The Floyd Press,* Floyd, Virginia, May 7, 2020.

13. Genesis 3:17–19.

14. Proverbs 24:30–31.

15. Second Corinthians 12:9.

16. John 16:33.

17. Elizabeth Barrett Browning, *Aurora Leigh*, ed. Kerry McSweeney (Oxford: Oxford University Press, 2008), 246.

18. Galatians 3:3.

19. Galatians 5:25.

20. Second Peter 3:3–4, 8–9.

21. Galatians 4:4 (ESV).

22. John 4:14.

23. John 7:38.

24. Robert Herrick, "To the Virgins, to Make Much of Time," in *The Cavalier Poets: An Anthology*, ed. Thomas Crofts (New York: Dover, 1995), 15.

25. Luke 12:27–28.

26. Luke 12:29–32.

27. Mary Oliver, "The Summer Day," in *New and Selected Poems* (Boston: Beacon Press, 2004), 94.

28. Matthew 16:2–3.

29. Matthew 13:14.

30. C. S. Lewis, "Is Theology Poetry?," in *The Weight of Glory and Other Addresses* (New York: HarperOne, 2001), 139.

31. Ecclesiastes 11:4–6.

32. John 4:37–38.

33. Psalm 96:12–13.

34. Wendell Berry, "Damage," in *World-Ending Fire: The Essential Wendell Berry* (Berkeley, CA: Counterpoint, 2019), 98, Kindle.

35. Isaiah 8:7–8.

36. Amos 5:8.

37. Jeremiah 8:7–8.

38. Psalm 147:15–17.

39. Psalm 147:18.

40. Isaiah 26:19.

41. First Corinthians 15:49 (csb).

42. Genesis 1:2.

43. Psalm 18:11.

44. Colossians 1:16–20. Line breaks added.

45. Matthew 6:25–26.

46. Matthew 10:28–31.

47. Isaiah 11:9 (csb).

48. Isaiah 10:33 (csb).

49. Annie Dillard, *Pilgrim at Tinker Creek* (New York: Harper Perennial Modern Classics, 2007), 178.

50. John 12:24–25.

51. Psalm 19:1–4.

52. Romans 8:20.

53. English philospher Thomas Hobbes used this phrase in his 1651 book, *Leviathan*, to describe mankind's life outside human society. The complete phrase is "and the life of man, solitary, poor, nasty, brutish, and short." Thomas Hobbes and Richard Serjeantson, *Leviathan* (Ware, Hertfordshire: Wordsworth Editions, 2014), 97.

54. Psalm 8:3–4.

55. Psalm 8:9.

More Praise for *Turning of Days*

Turning of Days delights, mesmerizes, and intoxicates. With gorgeous prose and rich insight, Anderson calls us to radically notice the world around us so that, in Annie Dillard's words, "creation need not play to an empty house." This is a rare book, full of truth and beauty, that gave me new eyes to see the world around me with all its complex revelations and luminous wisdom.

TISH HARRISON WARREN | Anglican priest and author of *Liturgy of the Ordinary* and *Prayer in the Night*

It's amazing how much we can learn from nature, if we have the eyes to look, and the patience to ponder. Hannah Anderson's beautiful meditations on creation help us appreciate the wonder that is all around us, and the unique insights creation provides into the character of God and the life of faith. Reading this book is like going on a long, refreshing walk in the woods—it nourishes your soul in ways you can't fully articulate.

GAVIN ORTLUND | Pastor and author of *Retrieving Augustine's Doctrine of Creation*

If, as the poets say, attention is a form of devotion, Hannah Anderson has given her readers a great gift in these pages. In *Turning of Days*, she has modeled the worship that begins by venturing out, bending down, and considering: the frost and the floods, the deer and the daisies, the seeds and cicadas. To attend to our glorious, groaning creation is to see the steady Hand that sustains life in all of its teeming and wild variety. "An entire cosmos designed to teach you faith," Anderson reminds. This lovely, meditative book deserves to be read slowly under the banner of the skies.

JEN POLLOCK MICHEL | Author of *A Habit Called Faith* and *Surprised by Paradox*

When you pick up and read *Turning of Days*, you might move faster than the pace of the book. That's not because the book is slow, instead it's likely we are poorly trained at what the Andersons are leading us towards. It's a book that, with some urgency, pulls you by the sleeve, jerking you back to what you've missed in your speed. The real joy of this book is seeing what they show you.

JOHN STARKE | Author of *The Possibility of Prayer* and pastor of Apostles Church Uptown in New York City

This book is an invitation to awaken the senses—sight, smell, touch, and hearing. It bids you leave behind the noise, the rush, the unforgiving concrete jungles and find a park or garden and sit awhile. Hannah weaves ancient biblical truths like parables, around her keen observations of the natural world her words a paintbrush displaying divine purpose and patterns. Nathan's gentle illustrations of the outdoor world they both evidently love make this book a garment of beauty, woven by skilled words, colored by skilled artists combining to bring awe and wonder that inspire worship.

GUY AND HEATHER MILLER | Leaders of Commission

This series of rich meditations teaches us how we might see God's hand in His bewildering, beautiful, marvelous, tragic creation. Hannah Anderson's reflections exemplify how someone steeped in the biblical revelation learns to read the natural revelation, finding these two books to be mutually illuminating. Her well-wrought prose and Nathan Anderson's delicate illustrations invite us to follow Christ's command to consider the lilies—and the spring peepers, the dirt, the fern, the cicadas, the hawk, the roadkill, the seed. This book is a trustworthy guide to the vital work of attending to God's presence in our places.

JEFFREY BILBRO | Editor-in-Chief of *Front Porch Republic*